KT-441-281

RIVER PHOENIX
A SHORT LIFE
BRIAN J. ROBB

Plexus, London

791.43 PHO

Learning
Resource Centre
Stockton
Riverside College

All rights reserved including the right
of reproduction in whole or in part in any form
Copyright © 1994 by Brian Robb
Published by Plexus Publishing Limited
26 Dafforne Road
London SW17 8TZ
First Printing 1994

British Library Cataloguing in Publication Data

Robb, Brian
    River Phoenix: Short Life
    I. Titile
    791. 43028092

ISBN 0 85965 214 9

Printed in Great Britain by Bath Press Ltd
Designed by Phil Smee

This book is sold subject to the condition that it shall
not, by way of trade or otherwise, be lent, re-sold,
hired out or otherwise circulated without the pub-
lisher's prior consent in any form of binding or
cover other than that in which it is published and
without a similar condition including this condition
being imposed on the subsequent purchaser

10 9 8 7 6 5 4 3 2 1

Acknowledgements

A book such as this cannot be completed - especially
within the time - without the help, patience and per-
severance of a lot of people.

Firstly, I'd like to thank my family for their
patience and understanding - my wife Brigid and
son Cameron, and my parents Jim and Anne, for all
their support over the years.

I'd like to thank George Fergus for his speedy and
sterling work in helping me research River
Phoenix's early TV credits and for cuttings and
tapes from the United States. Without George's
quick and accurate responses to my queries, the
whole project would have taken a lot longer. Also,
thanks are due to John Lavalle of Des Plaines, Illi-
nois, for his time spent over the library photocopier.

Thanks also to Jo Chumas for material relating to
Australian coverage of Phoenix's death and for her
encouragement.

For their help, hospitality and advice I'd like to
thank all at Plexus, especially Nicky Adamson, Sandra Wake and Terry Porter.

Major thanks are due to the British Film Institute,
particularly John Riley of Information and Library
Services, for promptness in dealing with queries and
for the generosity of his help. Also thanks are due to
the staff of BFI Stills, Posters and Designs. I must
also thank old colleagues at The London Film Festival, Sheila Whitaker and Chestnutt McInley for
information relating to Silent Tongue.The publishers
would like to thank the following for supplying
photographs: Jean Cummings/All Action Pictures;
Foto Blitz/All Action Pictures; Alpha Photographic
Press Agency; The Associates/C.I.C; British Film
Institute; Stephen Ellison/Katz Pictures/Outline;
Nancy Rica Schiff/Katz Pictures/Saga; Lance
Staedler/LaMoine/Katz Pictures; People in
Pictures; Rob Brown/Retna Pictures; Drew Carolan/
Retna Pictures; Nancy Ellison/Retna Pictures;
T.L. Litt/Retna Pictures; Lance Staedler/Retna
Pictures; Brian J Robb; the Ronald Grant Archive;
Stephen Ellison/Shooting Star/Scope Features;
D. Whitley/Shooting Star/Scope Features; Ron
Galella/Sygma; Syndication International. Cover
photograph by Lance Staedler/Retna

We would also like to thank the following news-
papers and magazines for their assistance in
research: The Daily Express, Empire, The Evening
Standard, Gay Times, The Guardian, The Independent on
Sunday, Interview Magazine, Just Seventeen, The Los
Angeles Times, The Mail on Sunday, The Modern
Review, The Monthly Film Bulletin, The National
Enquirer, New York Magazine, The New York Star, The
New York Times, People Weekly, Premiere (UK),
Premiere (US), Select, Sight and Sound, Sky
Magazine, The Spectator, Spin, The Sun, The
Times, TV Guide, Variety, The Village Voice, The Wash-
ington Post.

Film stills courtesy of: Columbia Pictures; Island
Pictures; Lorimar Film Entertainment; Lucasfilm;
New Line Cinema; Paramount Pictures; Tri-Star Pic-
tures; Universal Pictures; Warner Brothers; Saul
Zaentz Productions.

For accommodation and conversation, thanks to
Gary Leigh of DWB.

For tapes and hospitality, thanks to Mike Wingate
of C&A Video in Edinburgh.

And finally, for putting up with it all, thanks are
due to the staff at The Central Times in Edinburgh.

Brian J. Robb

RIVER PHOENIX

A SHORT LIFE

Contents

Introduction: The New James Dean?   7

1 Child of God   17

2 The Explorer   27

3 Rising Son   41

4 Teen Idol   59

5 Running For Oscar   75

6 Directions   95

7 Reaching Out   109

8 My Own Private Addiction   129

9 Downfall   141

Filmography   158

Introduction

THE 'NEW James Dean' was the label attached to River Phoenix almost as soon as the news of his sudden and unexpected death was released to the media on 31st October 1993. The world was perplexed. This screen idol was supposed to be vehemently anti-drug, pro-environment, and a supposedly clean living film star, who wouldn't so much as look at a Diet Coke. Yet he had died on the sidewalk outside The Viper Room at 8825 Sunset Boulevard, early on the morning of Halloween, apparently of a self-administered drug overdose.

River Phoenix seemed an unlikely candidate to have died early from drug abuse. He just wasn't the live fast, die young type - or at least so we believed. He was, at the time of his death, becoming a serious leading man, an actor with a brighter future ahead of him. He'd weathered the storms of being a child star, a teen idol and an adolescent actor, and now he was poised to reap the rewards of all his hard work with a series of adult roles that would undoubtedly have brought him even greater acclaim and moved him along a further step up the ladder of Hollywood fame and fortune.

Death in Hollywood - especially sudden, dramatic and unexpected death - is the stuff of tinseltown legends. It can turn perfectly ordinary actors and actresses into icons, martyrs and symbols of lost opportunities. All of these things happened to River Phoenix posthumously. A cult very quickly formed around the dead actor.

He became an icon of his generation. He was destined to be to the 1990s what James Dean was to the 1960s - the lost cinematic youth, the boy who never grew up, Peter Pan brought to life and caught by the glare of the movie camera. Phoenix had enough of the handsome yet vulnerable good looks and the back catalogue of moody photographs on posters plastered on assorted teenage bedroom walls to fuel a cult. The big difference between Dean and Phoenix, however, was that River Phoenix had already starred in

River Phoenix in contemplative mood.

nine movies at the time of his death and seemed destined to be one of the adult star names of the nineties.

The reactions to Phoenix's death were many and widespread. A shrine with flowers, candles, photographs and handwritten tributes appeared spontaneously on the sidewalk outside the Viper Club on the day of his death, and remained a place of pilgrimage for fans. Within days of his death, a proposal was put forward by students at Edinburgh University in Scotland to rename the Mandela building, named in honour of the African National Congress leader Nelson Mandela, after River Phoenix instead.

Edinburgh University Students Association President Quenton Sommerville said the signatures on a petition had been collected by two female students who felt that Phoenix was a more suitable hero for their generation than Mandela. 'They feel that his contribution in acting, on raising awareness of issues concerning our generation is strong enough to forgive his lapse of judgement as far as drugs are concerned,' said Sommerville.

Similarly, students at London's St Martin's College of Art, instituted an all-night vigil at the Cafe de Paris in Leicester Square on the night of 16th November, to honour Phoenix. A plaque commemorating his birth and death was designed and erected by graphic design students of St Martin's College of Art.

Video stores reported hoards of teenage girls descending upon unsuspecting managers demanding every River Phoenix title in the shop to rent for an evening of Phoenix watching and mourning. Fans would congregate in one another's houses and watch the tapes into the early hours, bemoaning the lost promise of River Phoenix.

He was also seen as a martyr to his causes - pro-environmentalism, anti-fur and anti-nuclear statements being common in his interviews. Holly Jensen, one of Phoenix's associates from his involvement in the group People for the Ethical Treatment of Animals (PETA), said: 'He was a very idealistic, kind, sensitive, wonderful person.'

Within weeks, different TV stations had screened River Phoenix movies like *My Own Private Idaho, Stand By Me , Explorers* and *Running On Empty* in tribute to the actor. Even the blockbuster *Indiana Jones and the Last Crusade*, scheduled as usual as a bit of holiday escapism at the Christmas after his death, was billed instead as a 'poignant reminder of the lost talent of River Phoenix'. Every Sunday Supplement throughout that November and into December 1993 took the opportunity to do a story on Phoenix, often launching into a broadside against the Hollywood drug culture or the Los Angeles Club scene.

River Phoenix wasn't a standard child actor or teen idol - his films always

River Phoenix in Running On Empty. *His moving portrayal of a seventeen-year-old boy torn between family loyalty and a musical career won him an Oscar nomination*

had something that little bit different about them that marked them out as more than the run-of-the-mill Hollywood entertainment. As his career progressed, Phoenix was showing great judgement in balancing his more independent film commitments, which allowed him to stretch himself more as an actor, and his mainstream film acting, which kept his name in the eyes of the public and Hollywood casting directors. From his feature film debut in Joe Dante's *Explorers* (1985), it was clear that River Phoenix was to be one of the more serious younger actors in Hollywood. His character of Wolfgang Muller was the most serious of the trio of teenage adventurers who feature in the movie, being a parody of the white-coated scientist. Played primarily for amusement, *Explorers* had no emotional centre, and so didn't allow its young actors to do much with their fairly straightforward roles.

It was on *Stand By Me* (1986) that Phoenix made his first dramatic

River Phoenix at the time of Running On Empty. *His commitment to the environment meant that he was an important role model for many young people.*

impact. This low-budget movie took everyone by surprise by becoming the sneaker hit of the year, packing cinemas around the world with audiences keen to see this warmly nostalgic tale of the adventures of four boys over a weekend as they set out to look for the body of a boy supposedly hit by a train. Directed by Rob Reiner, *Stand By Me* had an emotional intensity that sometimes threatened to turn into straightforward schmaltz, but the realism of the four male leads managed to pull the film back from the brink on several occasions.

Phoenix's portrayal of Chris Chambers is of a boy who is wiser than his companions, showing experience beyond his years. It was to be a trait of many of the early characters Phoenix was to play - maturity and responsibility had been thrust upon these characters early.

River Phoenix was also to explore several father-son relationships, most

Young people could identify closely with River Phoenix as his unconventional upbringing brought a particular naturalism to his screen persona.

of them unconventional. These films turned notions of rebellion on their head. In films like *The Mosquito Coast* (1986), *Little Nikita* (1988) and *Running On Empty* (1988) Phoenix's character is seen pursuing a desire for American 'normality' that had been denied by his unconventional parents. These narratives gave audiences a young hero whose form of rebellion was a desire to conform, to fit in with everyone else, to belong. This was not the rebellion of a James Dean who would rebel for rebellion's sake. Phoenix's roles allowed him to draw on his own unconventional real life experiences to bring some truth to the parts he was playing.

Phoenix's own strange background and upbringing was uncannily reflected in many of these films. Born to sixties drop-out hippy parents, Phoenix spent his early years travelling around South and Central America, before returning to the United States in 1977. From arrival in Florida, the family headed across country to California, Hollywood and fame and fortune for River Phoenix. It is no surprise, then, that he was excellent at playing the child of unconventional parents - whether mad idealists, sixties radicals or Russian spies. His own life was a series of paradoxes: the rich film star son of sixties liberals; the resourceful but essentially uneducated street kid; the clean living but drug taking film icon; the actor who dearly wanted to be a musician. He knew what it was like, in the broadest terms, to be an outsider, to have an unconventional upbringing, to have less-than-conventional parents, to be constantly on the move and to feel you have no secure roots or background. His real life escapades fed into his convincing on-screen portrayals. Audiences found it easy to believe in the emotional intensity that Phoenix portrayed in films like *The Mosquito Coast* and *Running On Empty*, because for Phoenix, it was all true.

The father figure was to be a continuing element in several more of Phoenix's films. Whether it was the shadow of Harrison Ford's fully grown Indiana Jones overlaid on Phoenix's youthful portrayal in the opening sequence of *Indiana Jones and the Last Crusade* (1989); Kevin Kline's Joey Boca in the black farce *I Love You To Death* (1990), which has Phoenix's Devo Nodd trying to kill his father figure, Joey, in order to secure the attentions of Joey's wife; William Richert (the director of *A Night in the Life of Jimmy Reardon*) as the cowardly chickenhawk in *My Own Private Idaho* (1991); or even Robert Redford as the leader of the high-tech gang in Phil Alden Robinson's ensemble thriller, *Sneakers* (1992), the father-figure was always present.

For so long in his career, this father-son connection (whether biological or symbolic) was to be the defining relationship of many of Phoenix's films, never quite allowing the actor to stand on his own two feet as a leading man. Yet towards the end of his life, Phoenix was beginning to secure more adult roles that would have allowed him to move onto the next phase of his acting life. In Nancy Savoca's *Dogfight* (1991), he had the only top-billing role of his

*River Pheonix was an intuitive actor, whose lack of
formal training was never a disadvantage.*

short career, as the mixed-up United States Marine Eddie Birdlace who falls for the plain Lili Taylor as Rose, after he takes her to the 'dog fight' of the title, a Marine ritual in which a prize is given to the person who brings the ugliest girl to the dance.

At the time of his death, Phoenix was playing in three ensemble movies. *The Thing Called Love* (1993) had received a limited release in the United States to a lukewarm critical and public reception. Phoenix stars as one of four Country and Western musician hopefuls who travels to Nashville hoping to hit the big time. The film, directed by Peter Bogdanovich, allowed Phoenix to indulge another of the great loves of his life - his music. He wrote and performed songs for the film, but these Country and Western tracks were very different from those performed by his progressive rock band Aleka's Attic, which was taking on more importance in the last few years of his life.

Phoenix was also to be seen in two more risky and unconventional projects. *Silent Tongue* (1993) was written and directed by American playwright Sam Shepard. The film features Phoenix as a husband driven mad in grief after the death of his half-Indian wife during childbirth. It's an unconventional role, and one which showed a new side to Phoenix's acting skills. The film was due for release after the actor's death.

Even more unusual was his role as Boy in George Sluizer's *Dark Blood* (1993). Phoenix was working on the film the day he died, and it is doubtful that the film will ever be completed without him. It was to tell the story of the encounter between two city types (played by Judy Davis and Jonathan Pryce) and a young man living rough (Phoenix).

Much of River Phoenix's short life was spent up on the cinema screen. He was an instinctive, intuitive actor who reached straight down from the screen into the hearts of millions. He was serious about his profession and serious about the world. Much respected in Hollywood, he was a young actor who gained the opportunity to work with many vastly experienced directors and actors. He was also part of an apparently close-knit family which, while spending many years on the road, prided itself on its self-sufficiency and cohesion. Indeed, his sister Rain was with him when he died. Yet it is clear that Phoenix's parents, by their own admission, deliberately engineered a screen career for their eldest son, and his innate talent soon made him the chief breadwinner. It is possible to see in this the roots of confusion, which, wrapped up with a careless, reckless side to his character, could have led to his downfall and death.

Chapter 1

THE FIRST public performance River Phoenix gave was his birth. Born to parents, John and Arlyn Phoenix, with strong beliefs in leading an alternative lifestyle, the birth of River Jude Phoenix was a totally natural event. Like something from a fairy tale, it all took place in a log cabin in Madras, Oregon on 23rd August 1970. Arlyn had invited several friends over from the commune in which they were living to witness the birth. The arrival of her first son was greeted with a 'roar of approval' from all who were there, she later said.

John and Arlyn had met in the late 1960s. Arlyn Dunetz was married to a computer operator and working as a secretary in Manhattan, New York. 'At eighteen I was just a clone, totally unconscious,' said Arlyn of her early life. 'I didn't know that the air was polluted and I didn't care. I just went to work and thought that everything the Government told me was right and true. It took some time before I awakened. I became aware. It was difficult because my parents weren't seeing the same things, but I knew I had to change my life.'

Leaving behind her job and her mother, Margaret Dunetz, Arlyn set out to travel to Los Angeles, hitch-hiking with a friend. She was determined to pursue the sixties promise of freedom and the ability to lead your life in any way you wished. However, having arrived in a new city with new prospects open to her, Arlyn still had no clear idea of what direction her life was going to take. Then fate intervened.

'I was hitchhiking on Santa Monica Boulevard and John picked us up,' said Arlyn of that first meeting with her future partner John, in 1968. 'He invited us up to his place and we went two nights later. We talked and talked till early morning and we just knew we had similar desires.'

John was a high school drop-out and self-styled poet and songwriter. His trades had included such manual occupations as furniture restoration and a period as a glazier. He was a year younger than 22-year-old Arlyn

River Phoenix's unconventional childhood gave him the
maturity to take on starring roles from the age of ten.

Dunetz. John had also been married before and had a daughter, named Trust. John, who has managed to keep his original surname a closely guarded secret (adopting the symbolically loaded surname of Phoenix in 1977 upon returning to the United States), was born in Fontana, California. An early magazine profile claimed that John had a history of 'juvenile homes and drinking problems', and had never revealed his original surname as he hated it so much. He was, like Arlyn, on the road, living out the sixties search for a meaning in his life. They called themselves 'seekers'.

Deciding that they had much in common in their attitudes to the world and aspirations in life, the pair travelled together, making money from casual jobs they picked up as they explored the western United States and indulged in the almost mandatory sixties recreational drug use, particularly LSD. While employed as fruit pickers on a commune in Madras, Oregon, Arlyn gave birth to their first son, named River Jude, with the River part of the unusual name being inspired by the river of life in Herman Hesse's cult novel *Siddhartha* (1922), which was enjoying a burst of popularity at that time. 'They just couldn't find their place in the city,' Phoenix later said of his parents. 'They found themselves living in Oregon, picking apples and living as close to nature as possible, and that's when I was born.'

Once Phoenix began his professional career, he felt his unusual first name became more acceptable, but during his childhood he had had reason to curse his parents for saddling him with a name like River. 'I would get songs sung to me, like Old Man River, or kids would call me Mississippi and things like that,' he recalled of his childhood days. 'At the time, I wished I had a name that blended in more with my surroundings. Now, though, I've really learned to love it. From fifteen I really liked it, it felt appropriate. Before that I don't think it quite fitted me. I had to grow into it.'

The family, now a threesome, continued to travel around the American West. Looking for direction in their lives, John and Arlyn joined the Children of God religious sect in Pikes Peak, Colorado and quickly renounced the sixties drug of choice, LSD.

The controversial evangelical religious cult Children of God was led by David Berg. He was a self-styled Messiah figure who capitalised on people like John and Arlyn Phoenix - 'seekers' who were looking for a way of life distinct from the mainstream and who were open to new ideas and new experiences. In turn John and Arlyn found the structure to their lives that they had been looking for - they now had a purpose, to spread the word of God.

While working as missionaries for the Children of God in Crockett, Texas, in 1973, Arlyn gave birth to their even more extravagantly named first daughter Rain Joan of Arc. Rain was later, at the age of eleven , to extend her first name to Rainbow, feeling that 'Rain' on its own was 'kind of dreary'.

River spent much of his childhood on the move, but he still had time for regular boyhood interests.

Rain recalls her childhood as a period when 'we used to sing and hand out pamphlets,' in South American shopping plazas.

The Phoenix family spent their early years in relative poverty, travelling around the country, evangelising on behalf of the Children of God and recruiting new members. The young River Phoenix saw nothing unusual in the peripatetic nature of his family life as he had nothing to compare it to. 'As a family, we've done a lot of moving around and a lot of changing. When you're born into that kind of lifestyle, you just don't even question it,' he was to say in later interviews.

The family travelled extensively, spreading the gospel according to Children of God sect leader David Berg throughout Central and South America. Following a stint in Mexico, the family were located in Puerto Rico, where Arlyn gave birth to her second son, and third child, Joaquin Raphael. By the age of four, Joaquin was to decide that he too wanted a 'nature name' like his brother and sisters, and so adopted Leaf as his first name. Phoenix commented: 'He picked it himself, after he saw Dad raking the leaves one day.' In the early 1990s he was to revert back to Joaquin once more.

By the time the family had reached Venezuela, John was trusted enough by the cult leaders to be appointed to the job of 'Archbishop of Venezuela and the Caribbean' for the Children of God. Phoenix was later to claim that his parents missionary work was undertaken 'not out of choice, but was more like a desperate situation'. Once they'd got involved with the cult they found it difficult to contemplate any other way of life.

Both Arlyn and John had been searching for some alternative stability to their lives than that offered by mainstream America. In the Children of God they had found just that, and for several years it was to provide the right, steady background within which they could put into practise their preferred lifestyle. In later years the accepting communities of Hollywood were to provide the same function for the Phoenix family. Both dubious religion and the American entertainment industry were to give their lives a purpose, while allowing the family to live in the manner they had chosen.

In Venezuela, Arlyn and John had a fourth child, a second daughter named Libertad Mariposa or Liberty Butterfly, who was born in Caracas on the fifth of July. The Spanish name was a deliberate choice, with most of the family, including the young River Phoenix being bi-lingual in Spanish and English. In fact, at that time Phoenix considered Spanish his first language and as a child he was known as Rio, the Spanish rendering of his first name.

Arlyn made every attempt to bring up her children according to her beliefs. The whole family practised veganism - complete avoidance of animal products, including dairy products - and maintained an avoidance of orthodox medicine. 'I've refused to have them inoculated,' she said later of her children. 'I've never given them an aspirin. If some awful illness happened in our family...then I'd look at it as a challenge to heal ourselves with herbs and spiritual enlightenment.'

After two years in different areas around South and Central America, the Phoenix family idyll was blown apart by magazine revelations about the lifestyle of David Berg, the Children of God cult leader. The family ended its association with the cult. 'The guy running it got crazy,' said Arlyn. 'He sought to attract rich disciples through sex. No way.'

River Phoenix also recalled the reason for the split, ascribing a more active role in the discovery of Berg's foibles to his own father. 'It was honest-to-goodness missionary work my parents were doing,' said Phoenix. 'They were Archbishops of South America just before we broke from the church. What happened was my dad started finding out stuff, getting into top secret categories, like that the leader was involved in fraud, a big hypocrite, and that this group wasn't as wholesome as they led people to believe. One day my parents just said "We're outta here".' (The cult continued to attract controversy right into the 1990s. Now known as The Family, 68 cult members were arrested in Buenos Aires in September 1993 on charges ranging from child abuse to kidnapping.)

Cut off from the protection and structure that the Church had provided to their lives, the family was reduced to making ends meet in any way they could. The six of them lived in a beach hut in Venezuela, awaiting guidance from a 'Universal Being' whom they believed would save them. River's idea of God was amorphous at best, but his experiences certainly led him to believe in some kind of superior being. 'I don't know if the superior being is in the form of a man, woman or jellyfish, but when I think of my parents and their different worlds and how they met and had kids, there has to be something up there.'

Phoenix was later vividly to recall this period of his life. 'When I was very young, we were stranded in Venezuela without any money. We lived in a shack on the beach that had no toilet and was rat infested - it was really horrible. But I was never frightened. When you're raised on the road you don't fear these things, you don't question them. We had faith, a lot of faith. When we didn't have enough money, we prayed and ate coconuts we found on the beach.'

It was this need to generate some kind of income that first led River Phoenix to public performing. The five-year-old River Phoenix and his three-year-old sister Rain were to be found singing and playing religious songs on the streets of Caracas, mainly outside hotels and at the airport to raise money for a passage back to the United States. 'It was a great stepping stone. I learned to play guitar there - my sister Rain and I got interested in performing. It was a neat time growing up in Venezuela in the late seventies.'

The family eventually made its way back to American in 1977. 'We met this doctor who used to be a pop star in Spain. He had a recording studio in Orlando, Florida and he told us we could come out whenever we wanted to. We had no money, so a priest got us on this old Tonka freighter that carried Tonka toys. We were stowaways. The crew discovered us halfway home - my mom was pregnant, there were four kids. They threw a big birthday party for my brother, gave us all these damaged Tonka toys. It was a blast.'

'When we finally made it to Florida, we stayed with my grandparents for a while, then moved to Central Florida. My sister and I pursued our interest in music, playing in talent shows and fairs. My dad was doing carpentry work.'

The family never expressed any regret concerning the years they spent travelling around Central and South America. The jaunt had provided the escape from the straight jacket of normal American life that both Arlyn and John

The Phoenix family at home. Left to right: River's youngest sister, Summer, his mother Arlyn, sister Liberty, brother Leaf (Joaquin), River's father John, Rain, and River.

had been looking for. They had headed off on an adventure with one child and returned with four; they had expanded their horizons and lived life their way.

In particular, Arlyn Phoenix was aware that the lifestyle they were leading was solely theirs by choice. No one else was to blame, and the outcome of it all was their responsibility: 'There were some hard times. I could have packed it in at any point. Even with the four kids, I could have said "I'm going to call my mother". My family is not wealthy, but they could always have come up with the $1000 air fare. It never came to that. There never seemed any alternative more interesting than the plan we were living. I can't imagine it any other way. I remembered the life I had lived in New York, as a secretary, shopping at Saks Fifth Avenue. I knew that my answers weren't there. There was never any question of going back or of what to do next.' Her philosophy of life was fairly simple: go with the flow, or as she was to put it:

'All will evolve.'

In interviews throughout his life, River Phoenix was to refer to all the benefits he felt he'd had from his highly unusual childhood. Yet it is possible to sense a defensiveness underlying the desperately positive statements. 'I love travelling,' he would say. Or, 'It was a learning experience. I got to be in new places, new atmospheres. It taught me to adapt. It's helped me with what I do as far as acting goes, you know, being able to blend in. It's given me a lot of insight, you know, like meeting different types of characters and stuff.'

He was also to emphasise the benefits of having parents who did not treated the younger members of the family as mere children, but as equals who had important contributions to make to the decision making process within the family.

River's early life gave him the resilience and experience to bring an unusually mature naturalism to his juvenile film roles, as here in Stand By Me.

'We never treated them like children but like extra added friends,' said Arlyn of her approach to child rearing on the road. 'And they have always held up their part of the deal. It was never like "We know better because we are the parents". It was more like "This is the first time we've ever done this too. What do you think?" And the children were so wise. If we made a mistake, we made it together. But if you open yourself up, a way presents itself. You find the right path.'

Phoenix confirmed that the relationship he and his brother and sisters had with their parents was important to the forming of their own beliefs and characters: 'We respect our parents and they respect us. Even when we were younger it was never, "Well, I'm the parent and you're the kid." Just the opposite. My father talks to Summer, who is the youngest, as he talks to my grandfather or anyone else. They always gave us a fair shot.'

This maturity beyond his years was to come through clearly in the acting roles that River Phoenix played early in his career. Critics were to find that Phoenix was the emotional centre of many of the early films, displaying a certainty that actors his age rarely have. But he had to grow up quickly, learning to deal with poverty and deprivation to an extent that his future contemporaries in Hollywood could never have imagined.

Arlyn Phoenix claimed she saw an inevitability in her children's success. Once the family was established as a show business entity, she said: 'This is more than show business to us. I really think there is a purpose why all of this is happening to us. We just have to be patient and let it find us. We've been blessed with five extraordinary children. I look at them at times and wonder why they're mine. The world's in such awful shape right now, maybe somehow we can make a difference. Life is all about finding reasons, all you have to do is open your heart...'

Chapter 2

ETURNING TO America in 1977 the family adopted the surname
Phoenix, in recognition of the fresh start they were planning for their
lives. Their involvement with the Children of God was behind them,
as were their travelling days. Now was the time for the family to settle and
find a new vocation.

In 1978, while father John was working regularly as a landscape garden-
er providing an income for the family, Arlyn Phoenix gave birth to her fifth
and final child, named Summer Joy.

Constantly asked about her children's names, Arlyn always had a ready
answer. 'River, Rainbow, Leaf, Liberty, Summer...those are all such beautiful
things. We just wanted to remind people of the beauty around them. Leaf
even chose his own name - we didn't give it to him. They can change them
anytime they wish. They could change them to Larry, I don't care.'

When the newest addition to the Phoenix family was only three months
old John injured his back and aggravated an old injury he'd sustained in a
car crash during his youth. This meant that the manual work he had been
pursuing during his adult life - fruit picking, gardening, carpentry - was no
longer open to him. The family were back in the United States, but they still
had no money and no clear prospects.

Inspired by the experiences and successes of River and Rain singing and
dancing for money on the streets of Caracas, Arlyn and John Phoenix felt it
might just be possible for their children to begin earning instead. Perhaps
they could have a future in show business? 'We had the vision that our kids
could captivate the world,' said Arlyn.

Local talent shows were soon inundated with entries from family members with the surname Phoenix. River Phoenix found himself in the position
of winning several talent contests, and began to believe his parents' ambitions for their children could become a practical reality. Arlyn became ener-
gised with this new plan for the Phoenix family - after all it wasn't any more

River, aged 12, as Wolfgang Muller the boy genius in Joe
Dante's sci-fi spoof, Explorers, his first starring role.

crazy than their South American adventures. 'By the time I was eight I could do what I wanted,' claimed Phoenix. 'I was given complete freedom. And I used it. If I couldn't have done what I did, and if I didn't have the support of my family I wouldn't be here today.'

It was clear from the start that like so many child stars, behind him was a committed showbiz mother, albeit overlaid with some sixties hippy philosophy. 'My mom is a huge driving force in my work,' River confirmed once he gained Hollywood stardom. 'She's very involved - my dad would rather have his privacy. I could say the same about everyone in my family: they don't want much to do with the media that surrounds me.'

One day, Arlyn was watching the comedy TV series *Laverne and Shirley* when she recognised actress Penny Marshall with whom she'd had a schoolgirl friendship back in the Bronx. She immediately wrote to Marshall about her talented children, enclosing cuttings from local newspapers covering River and Rain's talent show victories.

The letter was passed on to the Head of Talent at Paramount, who sent out what was a fairly standard reply to enquiries of this sort. However, it was enough encouragement for the Phoenix family to uproot themselves once more, this time in search of fame and fortune in Hollywood.

Phoenix recalled the letter from Paramount: 'They answered, "Yeah, we'd be happy to see your children. If you're ever out in California by all means look us up, but don't make a special trip". And so, of course, we just threw everything into the old station wagon and drove out to Burbank.'

So, not long after arriving back in the United States, the Phoenix family were on the road again. Their car was nine years old and had seen much better days - the back window wouldn't close at all. In an interview in *Life* magazine in 1987, by which time the family were in their 40th home in 20 years, John Phoenix recalled the impromptu decision to head West to California. 'I said to myself "What a crazy person you are!" But the stars were so bright. I felt it just had to be right.'

The plan was laid. The future of the Phoenix family lay in the entertainment business - the children would earn and the parents would manage their careers. First, Arlyn realised, she must find out all she possibly could about how Hollywood operated. With this in mind she cannily secured a job at NBC TV as secretary to Head of Talent, staying only long enough to gain an insider's knowledge of the business. 'I knew I had to learn about reading scripts and making the right choices,' she was to say later. 'Then I quit because I knew I could help my own kids.'

River Phoenix was going through his own learning process, too. 'I took a couple of improvisational courses when I was about ten years old, and that was just to get out of myself,' he recalled. 'I was really shy and timid. Our exercises were things like "Pretend that you are a washing machine - what kind of sounds would you make?" and then we'd race back and forth and gurgle. It wasn't really anything having to do with technique or anything. I've developed all that through experience.'

Phoenix was to remain touchy throughout his life about two topics in particular: his lack of a formal education and the constant press reports and innuendo that the children had been forced into show business by mercenary parents. Phoenix did attend school, but only fitfully and intermittently. He more often had home tutors and film set tutors, as required by law for child actors. 'We went to school. Besides, any good family would teach their children at home, above and beyond school. And as far as having our "career thrust upon us", that's bullshit. We wanted to make it, we all wanted to be entertainers and our parents did whatever they could to help us.'

'We know that people think stage parents are bummers,' admitted John Phoenix about the role he and Arlyn played in guiding the film careers of the Phoenix clan. 'The kids started growing so much that the biggest thing I can do now is help them do whatever they want. I'm learning to butt out.'

'I never felt pushed into acting,' said Phoenix. 'My parents sacrificed a lot to help us build our careers. I guess they felt that if there was any success it might help get our concerns across. First off, we all share the success. I'm the front man who's actually up there. I can speak my mind and share my thoughts and hope it will make a difference.'

The difference between the dream of life in Hollywood, home of the stars of the silver screen and the down-to-earth reality of the place came alive for Phoenix upon arrival in the town, looking - along with everyone else - for that big break into show business. 'We had a shitty little apartment in North Hollywood. No kids were allowed, so we had to hide in the closet when the landlady came around to inspect the place.'

If living conditions were far from luxurious, River and Rain Phoenix clung to their childhood optimism to see them through any difficult times, hoping they'd go straight from being talented unknowns onto immediate fame and fortune. 'I figured I'd play guitar with my sister and we would be on TV the next day. We were really naive,' Phoenix admitted.

Life for the whole Phoenix family during the early days in California had an uncanny resemblance to their experiences in South America - they were constantly on the move, constantly short of money and constantly hustling - not pushing dubious religion this time, but trying to convince agents and casting directors how talented the Phoenix kids were.

'We schlepped forever in LA. Moved every three months, being evicted regularly for late rent, for kids, for whatever. We just kept it so we'd rather be poor than have any debts, but we had no money whatsoever - it was just day to day,' said Phoenix of his days trying to secure acting roles. But he did have an agent working for him. Iris Burton was to handle Phoenix's professional career for most of his acting life. 'They came to me when they were little children, the whole family. I've had them [on the books] since River was nine. He was the most beautiful child you've ever seen, like a little Elvis,' she said.

At last River was signed up for a series of commercials, including spots for Ocean Spray, Saks and Mitsubishi. But he was never comfortable in the world of TV commercials: 'Biggest problem was I was terrible for commercials - I couldn't smile on cue.' His ethical and political sensibilities were also developing at this time, resulting in growing doubts about using himself to push consumer products. After the fourth commercial, the eco-sensitive *wunderkind* rebelled. Legend has it that River Phoenix made the move into television drama after sitting his parents down and telling them that he was no longer happy with his commercial activities and had loftier acting goals in mind.

'I wasn't sure of anything,' Phoenix said of his growing awareness that commercials were not something he wanted to stick at for long. 'I guess what I was zeroing in on was that performing was more about telling the truth through a different character's eyes. I felt that the constant lying, the smiling on cue and the product-naming was going to drive me crazy or numb me to a not-yet-developed craft that I was beginning to feel staring me in the face.' His agent Iris Burton had to redirect his newly developing career. 'They said they wouldn't do commercials, because they were vegans. I said, "What the hell's a vegan?" I thought it was an alien. I said, "So, I guess you won't do Kellogg's commercials. I guess you won't do MacDonald's."'

At the age of ten Phoenix hit the LA TV audition circuit with a vengeance. Chaperoned around from try out to try out by one or other of his parents, usually father John, Phoenix found himself making friends with some of the other child actors whom he met at auditions, even though they were competitors for the same roles. One of them was Corey Feldman, with whom Phoenix was later to star alongside in *Stand By Me*.

'We were in competition at the same auditions,' said Feldman of his early meetings with Phoenix. 'We got to know each others families. He was a normal kid. We were both normal kids who were in the business.'

River Phoenix's first job in television came in 1980. Despite hankering after on-screen success, this first role was off-screen, as a studio audience warm-up performer, with his sister Rain, for a TV show called *Real Kids*. That led on to on-screen appearances strumming his guitar in the children's television show, *Fantasy*, also in 1980. Both these early roles depended upon Phoenix's musical abilities, with him playing guitar and he and Rain singing, rather than any developing acting skills.

But at last Phoenix struck lucky at an audition for a part in a TV series spin-off from the 1954 film *Seven Brides For Seven Brothers*. The musical film,

River Phoenix (centre) with the cast of the TV series Seven Brides for Seven Brothers. River played Guthrie MacFadden, the youngest of the seven brothers.

directed by Stanley Donen, was an unlikely choice for a TV series spin-off in the 1980s. The film had featured Howard Keel, whose decision to get himself a wife provokes his siblings to do the same. Renowned for its lively and colourful song and dance numbers, the film was also to become a Broadway musical as well as the short-lived 1982-83 TV series.

River Phoenix was cast as Guthrie McFadden, youngest - at age twelve - of the seven brothers. The TV series was updated to take place in 1982 and followed the farming rivalries in the Californian town of Murphy, as the brothers attempt to keep their ranch going despite perilous financial difficulties.

Phoenix's character of Guthrie was the denim clad, spirited and cheeky kid of the extended family, often providing the light relief. The opening episode has one of the brothers, Adam (Richard Dean Anderson) marrying Hannah (Terri Treas, later to star in the TV series *Alien Nation*). Acceptance into this family isn't easy, but Hannah quickly makes her mark and draws the siblings into accepting her as one of the clan. Much singing, dancing and many raucous meal times later, the McFaddens are competing in the local County Fair, trying to win a prize bull which will help the fortunes of their farm. Part of the Fair includes a pie-eating contest, into which young Guthrie is entered. The sequence uncannily echoes the fantasy story of Lardass and the pie eating contest told by Wil Wheaton's character to Phoenix in the later film *Stand By Me*. When the donor of the prize bull tries to withdraw it at the end as he doesn't want the McFaddens to win it, a fight breaks out between the McFadden boys and the local henchmen. Phoenix's Guthrie holds his own in the fight, until he unfortunately ends up in the pig sty.

River Phoenix featured in all of the 22 episodes of the series, which ran from September 1982 through to March 1983, as well as popping up during the title sequence announcing the return of the other brothers to the farm after a hard days work. Although the part was hardly challenging for the young actor, a regular role on a TV series, however short lived was a major step forward. Now he'd have something substantial to put on a show reel and tout around Hollywood's film casting agencies.

Looking back, River Phoenix was to have a less than high opinion of his work on the series, but he did realise the importance that securing his first regular TV role had for his early career. 'It seems like repetitious crap now,' he was to say, 'but then a series was big.' And indeed, following his exposure on *Seven Brides For Seven Brothers* which finished its run in March 1983, River Phoenix secured a host of TV appearances, from fairly minor guest spots to playing important characters in TV mini-series.

He popped up in *Celebrity* (NBC) in 1984, playing Jeffie, aged eleven , son of Joseph Bottoms' Mac Crawford. *Celebrity* followed the fortunes of three high school buddies - played by Ben Masters, Michael Beck and Joseph

Bottoms - from the 1950s through to the mid-seventies. One becomes a star actor, another an acclaimed journalist and the third a fraudulent evangelical preacher. The series opens with a shooting between the three - one is dead, one is in a coma and one did the shooting, but until the end of the series, structured as a series of long flashbacks, the audience doesn't know which of the trio pulled the trigger, which is dead and which is having the flashbacks.

Effectively realised, from the novel by Tommy Thompson, *Celebrity* featured Phoenix in the second of its three parts, when Jeffie witnesses his actor father in a homosexual liaison. It was a small part in a sprawling drama, but it was enough to continue to bring in TV work for Phoenix, including contributions to an after-school educational special on dyslexia called *Backwards: The Riddle of Dyslexia*.

Later in 1984 he appeared in the first few minutes of a pilot for a proposed NBC series, *It's Your Move*, starring Jason Bateman. Phoenix played Brian, delivering only one line of dialogue. Phoenix was to encounter Bateman again playing alongside him as one of Robert Kennedy's children in the 1985 mini-series *Robert Kennedy and His Times*. Phoenix played Robert Kennedy Jr, alongside future *Beverly Hills 90210* star Shannon Doherty as his sister Kathleen. Phoenix only appeared in the third episode of this seven hour drama, and tends to get lost among the other junior members of the Kennedy brood.

The series was a drama documentary, featuring much original archive footage and still photograph montages chronicling the years from 1946 when John F. Kennedy first ran for Congress to June 1968 when Robert Kennedy was assassinated in the Ambassador Hotel in Los Angeles by Sirhan Sirhan.

The final episode, which features Phoenix in those scenes aiming to illustrate Robert Kennedy as family man, chronicles Kennedy's campaign trail for the Presidency in 1968, through the shooting of Martin Luther King to his own assassination. It was a heavy-weight mini-series which did no harm to Phoenix's list of minor TV credits.

In the same year, Phoenix featured as a guest star in an episode of *Family Ties*, the long-running Michael J. Fox series. He played a thirteen-year-old math whiz-kid (although he was fifteen at the time) who is brought in to tutor Fox's Alex in an attempt to improve his grades - only to spend his time pursuing Alex's sister, Jennifer (Tina Yothers).

River Phoenix's final starring TV role was in the 1985 TV movie, *Surviving: A Family In Crisis*, broadcast on ABC on 10th February 1985. He played the brother of Zach Galligan (who starred in Joe Dante's *Gremlins* (1984), just as Phoenix was to go on and star in Dante's *Explorers*), a teenager who fulfils a suicide pact with his girlfriend, Molly Ringwald. Acclaimed by *TV Guide* for its 'tour-de-force performances', the socially aware drama made a big splash, putting the spotlight on all the participants.

Although the finished product featured a polished performance from the young Phoenix, it hadn't been that easy for the young actor to meet the expectations of others - particularly his father, who was his chaperone on the *Surviving* set. Director Waris Hussein was aware of at least one instance where parental intervention was involved in drawing a performance from Phoenix. 'His father took him aside,' said Hussein. 'It was done in a very quiet way, but I could sense that there was a lot of "you'd better get this right" sort of attitude. It's a very subtle form of authority. They [River's parents] were very anxious for him to succeed.'

Even as a young teenager, River Phoenix's peripatetic lifestyle had an influence on his preferred career moves. While a starring TV series role was definitely on the cards by now, Phoenix chose not to pursue that option. 'Some people find security in routine, but I could never live that way,' he said. 'That's why I could never be on a television series; that would call for routine, for getting up in the morning at a certain time, going to work, going through the same thing, playing the same character.'

Phoenix was back on the audition trail - but for feature films rather than TV roles. He now had an impressive show reel, including guest spots on *Hotel* (ABC). This process was to lead him to securing one of the leading roles in a major feature film.

Joe Dante's *Explorers* (1985) is the tale of three adventurous kids who receive messages in their dreams, instructing them on how to build a spaceship. The three kids are, for one reason or another, misfits at school and they team up to put into action the plan which is being beamed at them from outer space. After this extended prologue, the trio of adventurers achieve lift off, only to be gobbled up by a huge organic-looking mothership. Inside they discover two wonderfully wacky rubber aliens, who are big fans of Earth junk culture. Expecting to discover the secret of the universe, the trio instead come across alien couch potatoes, one of whom admits: 'I watched four episodes of *Lassie* before I figured out why the little hairy kid never spoke. He could roll over fine - he could do that - but I didn't see he deserved a series for that!'

Communication is impossible between the Earth children and the aliens, who endlessly quote a melange of film dialogue randomly picked up from television, including W C Fields, Marilyn Monroe and Bugs Bunny. The final twist in the story comes when we discover that the aliens are themselves errant children, and the bigger, brasher parent aliens turn up to send the Earth kids packing and take their own brats home for a good telling off.

'The film is primarily about believing in something enough to be able to make it happen,' said director Joe Dante of *Explorers*. 'This is a story about three kids and how they try to make their dreams come true.'

Dante, a protégé of the Roger Corman school of cheap, cheerful and quick movie making, had enjoyed a major success with *Gremlins* (1984), a blackly comic tale about furry little critters that manage to destroy a small American town at Christmas time. Graduating from Philadelphia's college of art, Dante began his filmmaking career in 1974 cutting together film trailers for Roger Corman movies. It wasn't long before Corman gave the ambitious young man in a hurry a chance to direct.

Dante was a big fan of forties and fifties science fiction films and this love of the genre infuses *Explorers*. One of the characters is seen watching fifties SF films, including *War of the Worlds* (1953) and *This Island Earth* (1954). Later in the film, the aliens use clips from classic science fiction movies like *The Day The Earth Stood Still* (1951) to indicate how they fear aliens are treated on Earth.

The film was the screenwriting debut of Eric Luke, who graduated from UCLA film school in 1978 but had come up with the idea for the story while working at the LA fantasy bookstore, A Change of Hobbit. Luke was an aspiring actor (who pops up in a cameo role in *Explorers*), who had held var-

On the receiving end of school bullying, River Phoenix as Wolfgang Muller fights back with words rather than violence in Explorers (1985).

ious Hollywood jobs, including a low point hoisting the dialogue cue cards for the daytime soap *Days of Our Lives.*

'I remember driving home one night and looking up at the full moon. All of sudden this feeling came - why not build your own spaceship? When I was a kid I used to have a lot of the same dreams that the three explorers share. Writing the script was a way of making it all come true.'

Luke actually completed his script in the spring of 1983, but failed to generate any interest from the Hollywood studios. It was a pair of independent producers, Edward S. Feldman and David Bombyk who saw the possibilities in the project. 'The first 60 pages of the script were simply an extraordinary, unique idea,' said Feldman.

Finding three actors to carry off the pivotal leading roles in *Explorers* was a difficult task for casting director Susan Arnold. She launched a nationwide talent search and over a period of three months she saw 4000 boys for the parts, all aged between twelve and fourteen, before narrowing the choices down to River Phoenix, Ethan Hawke and Jason Presson. Hawke was the only one with no acting experience - Phoenix had his television background and Presson had made his film debut in *The Stone Boy* the previous year.

Dante saw a potential in River Phoenix that led him to swap the actors and their intended roles around. 'River originally came in for the kid from the other side of the tracks [played by Presson]. But we wanted River to do the scientist kid. It was a kind of a nerd character, and this was the last thing he would ever want to be. It was a tribute to his acting chops that he said "Okay". He had to wear glasses and cut his hair short. Whenever there were girls around he would quickly take the glasses off and try to look cool.'

Inside their home-made capsule, the three youthful stars of Explorers. Left to right: Ethan Hawke, River Phoenix and Jason Presson.

There were difficulties for Joe Dante in working with three children as the leads in a major film production. The State of California Child Labour Laws state that anyone under the age of eighteen is considered a legal minor, therefore cannot be allowed to work in excess of four hours each working day. On top of that, film producers must schedule in a legally-required three hour period of schooling, with another hour set aside for lunch and a further full hour's worth of rest breaks. And the laws are rigidly enforced.

'Some days you just give up,' said Dante. 'You might be in the middle of a shot and suddenly it's time - the kids have to go home. They might even be willing to stay, but it doesn't work that way.'

Dante knew the problems, though, and was undaunted in his task of producing a thoroughly entertaining film. 'I love working with kids. In some ways, working with children is much more rewarding than working with adults, because the acting goes through much less filtering.'

Identifying the approach to acting that Phoenix was to maintain throughout his acting life, Dante felt that kids were much more 'natural' on the big screen. 'Adults will think very hard about a scene - intellectualise - and it ruins the spontaneity. Kids will frequently come up with something that just cuts right through and is so real.'

Production on the film began on 15th October 1984 on locations in Petaluma, California, about 40 miles north of San Francisco. This location, in the heart of Sonoma County, was close to the headquarters of Industrial Light and Magic (ILM) , the special effects company set up by George Lucas after the success of the *Star Wars* series of films. ILM, located in neighbouring San Rafael, was to provide the special effects sequences for the film and were

Wolfgang Muller (River Phoenix) exploring the interior of the alien space craft in Explorers.

credited as co-producer. Production continued right through to February 1985 (when Phoenix's role in *Surviving: A Family in Crisis* aired on TV), in the studios at Paramount and on location in the Los Angeles area.

The three leads found themselves spending much time together on the film, and Phoenix and his co-stars were not adverse to a little ad-libbing, either. 'One of the boys would come up with a line that was funnier than one in the script,' said novice screenwriter Luke, 'I didn't feel put out by it at all. Joe and I would look at each other and say "Why didn't we come up with something that good?"'

The three young actors all received good notices in the press upon the film's release, both in the United States and the UK. *The New York Times* called the film 'eccentric...charmingly odd', describing the three main characters as 'a smart-alecky one, Jason Presson; a scientific wizard, River Phoenix, and the obligatory nice-looking straight-arrow, Mr Hawke.'

Britain's *Daily Express* called Phoenix 'engaging' in one of the leading roles, commenting that the film was 'wonderfully bizarre.' The London

Joe Dante directs River Phoenix and his alien friend on the set of Explorers. Joe Dante found River Phoenix was a natural screen actor.

Evening Standard concentrated on Phoenix's character at the centre of the film: 'The brainiest boy - a child of German immigrants who's allowed to sit up late in his home laboratory just by mentioning Werner Von Braun - discovers an anti-gravity force and builds a spaceship for three in the old junk yard.' However, the $20 million film was not a hit in the United States and faded from screens after about two weeks. As a result, release in the UK was delayed by over a year. In fact, *Explorers* was already available on video prior to its Christmas 1986 limited release in Britain. With the video release, the film did begin to find an appreciative audience both in the UK and the United States, and Joe Dante still considers *Explorers* to be one of his own favourites among the films he's made.

For River Phoenix, *Explorers* was the stepping-stone into the world of feature films, leaving behind the guest spots and thankless roles in television commercials and series. However, the film was just a warm up for the young actor, as his next two films were to clearly show him to be an acting talent to be reckoned with.

Chapter 3

RIVER PHOENIX went straight from wrapping production on *Explorers* to being cast in the central role of Chris Chambers, the thirteen-year-old from the wrong side of the tracks, in Rob Reiner's *Stand By Me*. Phoenix was one of over 300 young Hollywood hopefuls who auditioned for the central four roles in a film which, like *Explorers*, would depend upon its youthful leads to make it work successfully.

River Phoenix originally read for the leading role in the movie, that of sensitive aspiring writer Gordie Lachance, eventually filled by Wil Wheaton. Phoenix was the oldest of the leading quartet, turning fifteen during the summer of 1985, but ended up playing the part of Chris Chambers - the film's mediator and peacemaker.

'River has all the strength that the character of Chris Chambers has,' said director Rob Reiner. 'It's clear he's been loved by his parents, who are people who have been able to maintain what was good and pure about sixties morality without the garbage.'

In taking on the film, Phoenix saw enough echoes in the role and the emotions of the characters from his own life that he knew he could make a success of what was his most challenging role to that time. 'The movie is about friendship,' he said, 'and how you need to have faith that you can do better in the future than you have in the past.'

Stand By Me chronicles one weekend in 1958 in the lives of four friends - Gordie Lachance (Wil Wheaton), the young aspiring writer whose football jock brother (John Cusack in flashback cameos) has recently died, rendering Gordie invisible to his heart-broken parents; Chris Chambers (River Phoenix), the kid from a bad family, already labelled a failure in life due to his background, despite being intelligent and smart; Teddy Duchamp (Corey Feldman), the reckless, disfigured kid who still believes his father is a war hero, despite the fact that he's locked up in the 'loony bin', and Vern Tessio (Jerry O'Connell), the stereotypical fat kid with the courage deficiency.

River Phoenix as Charlie Fox in The Mosquito Coast. By the age of fifteen, River was already an object for teenage daydreams.

These four likely lads set out for a weekend's camping, on the trail of a kid's body rumoured to be in the woods by the railway track where he was hit by a train. Following close behind are a gang of older teenagers (led by Kiefer Sutherland as Ace), two of whom originally found the body, but were out driving in a stolen car at the time, so can't tell anyone except their mates. All the parties have hopes that their finding the body will lead to local fame and even a reward.

For Lachance, the search for the dead body is a way of dealing with his brother's death. For the others, it's the end of their final summer before serious schooling takes them in different directions in life. Chambers has to decide whether to give into the label attached to him by teachers and guidance counsellors. He knows there's little hope for the other two, Teddy and

The first of several campfire scenes to feature in River Phoenix's short film career, with the gang from Stand By Me (1986). Left to right: Wil Wheaton, River Phoenix, Jerry O'Connell and Corey Feldman.

Vern, but Gordie manages to convince Chambers that he too can do better for himself than the route through life that has been mapped out for him.

The film is a flashback, framed by the grown-up Gordie Lachance (Richard Dreyfuss). In a sadly ironic echo of Phoenix's own demise, he reflects on the events in the film upon his hearing of the early death in a stabbing incident of Chris Chambers, who'd become a successful lawyer despite his background.

The nostalgia-driven plot is wrapped up in late fifties music, from the title track by Ben E. King, (successfully re-released at the time the movie came out), to a whole selection of then-contemporary popular music. Also thrown in are references to TV series, such as *Dragnet* and *Wagon Train* ('Did you ever notice that they never get anywhere? They just keep on wagon training,' says Wheaton's Lachance) to cartoon characters ('If Mickey's a mouse, Donald's a Duck and Pluto's a dog, what's Goofy?'). The realistic banter of the kids, from the hesitant swearing to the put-on acts of sexual knowledge drives what is basically an episodic drama to its conclusion.

Phoenix performed beyond expectations in the film, showing much more promise than his role in *Explorers* had allowed. He seems more natural than the others, with Corey Feldman in particular exhibiting a tendency to overact and scene-steal. Phoenix's performance is quieter, more considered. Already in *Stand By Me* he is coming over on screen as wise beyond his years, showing a deeply embedded sense of authority, of rightness. He serves as a guidance counsellor to the other kids, with Gordie Lachance the only one who can give him advice in turn. The very effective performance from River Phoenix was only a hint of the things to come. 'He didn't have a lot of technique – you just saw this kind of raw naturalism,' Rob Reiner has said. 'You just turned the camera on, and he would tell the truth.'

Stand By Me was the third feature film directed by former TV comedy

The stars of Stand By Me pose for publicity shot on a camera crane. This was the nearest that River (right) got to fulfilling his ambition to direct films.

actor Rob Reiner. Son of comic writer-director-actor Carl Reiner, Rob Reiner first found fame as Archie Bunker's son-in-law on *All In The Family*, eight years before he turned, like his father before him, to directing movies. Reiner's first directorial effort was *This Is Spinal Tap* (1984), a well-judged spoof rockumentary following the fortunes of an absurd British heavy metal band. He followed that with *The Sure Thing* (1985), a romantic comedy following the ups and downs of two college students, starring John Cusack and Daphne Zuniga.

'Initially, what attracted me to *Stand By Me* was the intelligence of the writing in the original story,' Reiner explained. 'The characters were very strong and very well drawn. At the time I was looking to do something a little more dramatic, something different from the things I'd done in the past. I called the author, Stephen King, because I assumed that the piece was semi-autobiographical, or at least gave some hints to what led him to become a writer.'

Reiner took the basic material and overlaid some of his own personal concerns. 'While I felt I was examining what had made King the writer he is, I also injected my own personal feelings: what made me become what I am? I basically turned a lot of Gordie into me, a youth who feels he's not understood, with a lot of doubts and fears about himself, who through the help of a friend, starts to feel good and have confidence in himself. For both King and myself, the story was a lot more than just four boys searching the woods for a body.'

Before beginning to film, Reiner took his leading cast members, the writers and some members of his crew to a hotel in Oregon to play theatre games based on Viola Spolin's *Improvisations for the Theatre*. 'Theatre games develop trust among people, and her book is the bible,' said Reiner, explaining his unusual approach to rehearsals. Reiner had formed an improvisational theatre group with his friend Richard Dreyfuss when they were both 19.

For a week the central members of the cast got to know each other, to feel familiar with each other, comfortable in each other's presence - to become real friends. It was only in the second week that the cast began to work on read throughs of the actual script for the film. 'When you saw the four of us being comrades, that was real life, not acting,' said Wil Wheaton of the on-screen rapport between the four youthful leads.

Phoenix told Aljean Harmetz of *The New York Times* how he approached the fun of the improvisations before shooting and the actual chore of making the movie. 'The first three weeks were the most fun. We took all the hotel pool chairs and threw them in the pool. We soaked Corey's clothes in beer and they dried and he smelled like a wino. Wil Wheaton is a video whiz - he fixed the machines in the hotel so we got free games.'

'Just like in the movie we had big fights,' admitted Phoenix. 'Stupid stuff

- boys and their egos, like who got to walk down the railroad tracks first. Always, towards the end of a movie, you get sick of each other.'

Reiner used his acting experience to give the boys guidance as to the emotional pitch of each scene, coaxing the actors into giving as natural performances as possible. 'Rob would act out each character,' said Phoenix. 'I talked about the whole history of Chris with Rob. I decided he was older, thirteen, and had flunked one grade.'

For River Phoenix, shooting *Stand By Me* meant a return to the State of his birth. Filming began in Eugene, Oregon, near Madras where Phoenix had

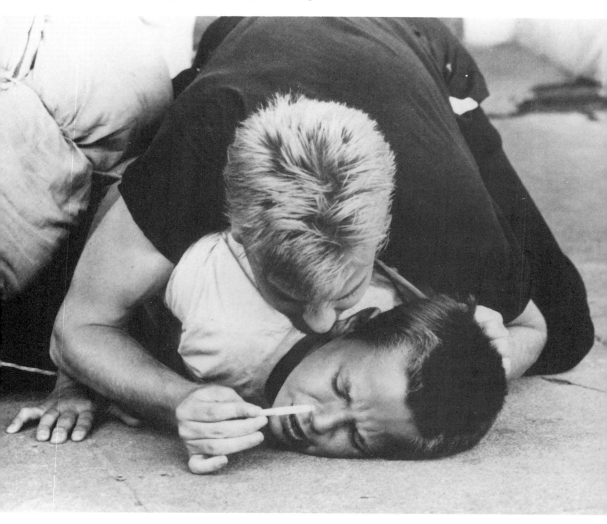

Kiefer Sutherland (as Ace Merrill) gets the upper hand in his conflict with River Phoenix (as Chris Chambers) in Stand By Me.

been born. Also used was the historic town of Brownsville, which was - with very few changes - converted to represent the fictitious town of Castle Rock, where many of Stephen King's stories are set. Enjoying an unusually hot and dry summer, the production began on 17th June 1985. In August, the film crew moved to the Mount Shasta area of California for a further two weeks of filming to capture the tricky scene where the boys traverse a railway viaduct with a train breathing down their necks.

Stand By Me was what Hollywood regards as a 'sleeper' success, meaning that the film was a small scale, inexpensive production, which slowly but surely became one of the year's biggest earners at the box office. After two weeks on only sixteen screens nation-wide, the film had made over $600,000 in the US. Distribution spread to 715 screens, with income reaching $3.8 million and a placing at number 2 in the national box office charts. After four weeks, $5 million had been spent by filmgoers to see *Stand By Me*, and this quiet, nostalgic film reached number one in the national box office chart, above the flashy and expensive Tom Cruise vehicle, *Top Gun* (1986).

The New York Times noted the 'extraordinary ensemble acting on the part of four eleven to fourteen year old actors,' in the film, while *The Village Voice* felt the credit for the performances lay with the director: 'Reiner elicits top notch performances from his young actors. All four manage to be tender and

River Phoenix had originally auditioned for the part of Gordie Lachance (Wil Wheaton, right) but his portrayal of Chris Chambers was remarkably thoughtful for his age and experience.

raunchy, sensitive but not dear, and thoroughly enraptured by their own boy-talk.'

Off-screen the four actors playing the leads in *Stand By Me* also did a lot of growing up. For Corey Feldman, *Stand By Me* was a film of many firsts. 'I smoked pot on that film for the first time, and I drank for the first time ever.'

For his part Phoenix claimed to have lost his virginity during the making of the film, although according to Feldman, Phoenix was getting into more than sex this early in his life. 'I went into his room and I saw a joint and he said, "Oh, it was someone else's..." I had been doing it too, but it was one of those things where we didn't really want to let each other know what we were doing.'

Director Rob Reiner would later take great pleasure in recounting the tale of the night River Phoenix lost his virginity. 'He was fourteen and his hormones are raging, and he was always saying "I want to meet a girl". Apparently he showed up to work one morning and had this big smile on his face; the night before he'd lost his virginity. A friend of the family – I think she was about eighteen – took River out into the backyard where they tented out. He said, "She was very patient with me and told me what to do." I thought, this may be the greatest story of lost virginity I've ever heard."' It would appear that Phoenix's first sexual experience was just one more facet of the young actor's life that was a family affair.

The almost overnight success of *Stand By Me* made River Phoenix a Hollywood name. Phoenix was aware that his work on the film would have a life beyond its immediate cinema release. 'In *Stand By Me* I realised that what I was creating was going to live on far longer than anything of me as a person. The characters are more powerful than the person that creates them.'

The young but successful actor was determined not to let his sudden fame go to his head. 'You see people you work with closely change every day and get really selfish. Like, I've been getting acclaim for *Stand By Me*. People say, the movie's so good, you're going to be the next this or the next that...Take it the wrong way and you can get really high on yourself. You get pampered. You hang out at a ritzy hotel, get room service at the snap of your fingers, or have a limo, which is really weird. You start expecting special treatment from other people. You get snobby and don't have time for the fans on the street who respect your work and want some contact. Or you start saying, "Oh, this friend isn't good enough for me because he's not in the business. I'll have to be friends with someone who's more important." You can change, and it's sad.'

As if foreshadowing his final few years, Phoenix was also aware of the deceptions of appearances: 'People get so lost. They think they have everything under control, and everything's out of control. Their lives are totally in pieces.'

The pampering and five star hotel treatment that River Phoenix feared was part and parcel of being a star was not to cause him any problems on his next film, *The Mosquito Coast* (1986), directed in the jungles of Belize by Australian film director Peter Weir.

The Mosquito Coast is the story of one man's folly in attempting to realise his skewed dream. Allie Fox (Harrison Ford) is driven by a desire to escape the modern world, to go with his family to an untainted, pure, jungle utopia, far from the corrupting influences of modern American life. He finds it's a utopia that exists only in his imagination.

Fiercely independent, Fox is fed up with modern American life, with fast food culture, vacuous television entertainment, environmental pollution, phony evangelism and ever increasing crime and violence. This world view reflected River Phoenix's own life view: 'In my Utopic world, I'd live on a tropical island without any industrialisation or pollution,' he said later. 'I'd be able to fly up to a mountain range nearby where there was snow, then make a sled out of an old stump and ski down the mountain to the bottom where I could bathe and swim in a running river and meet up with a group of friends.' Like Allie Fox in *The Mosquito Coast* he appeared unconscious of the paradox involved in this statement. In the film, the Harrison Ford character packs up his wife, two sons and twin daughters, and boards a freighter bound for the Mosquito Coast, which extends from Puerto Barrios in Guatemala to Colon in Panama. *The Mosquito Coast* is the story of how one family's quest for paradise turns into a desperate battle for survival.

The driving force to turn Paul Theroux's novel *The Mosquito Coast* into a film was producer Jerome Hellman, who had read it in 1982 and bought the film rights personally shortly after the book was published. 'Very rarely do you read something that gets you really excited,' said Hellman of his attraction to the unusual material. 'I felt it could make a wonderful movie if the right people were involved.'

Writer-director Paul Schrader, the man behind the controversial film *Taxi Driver*, was engaged by Hellman to adapt the book into a screenplay, which was finished in 1983. Hellman had begun talking to director Peter Weir about tackling the film, based on his previous works such as *Picnic At Hanging Rock* (1975), *The Last Wave* (1977) and *The Year of Living Dangerously* (1983).

'The thematic harmony between Peter's previous work and *The Mosquito Coast* was striking,' said Hellman. 'I was also impressed with the humanism of his work - this was not a man with a cynical attitude towards people or towards life.' The package - of Schrader's script and Peter Weir attached to direct - did the rounds of the Hollywood studios, and despite being approved for production several times, it was to be many more years before the film actually got underway. 'No sooner had an executive approved us for production.' said Hellman of the delays, 'than he or she headed elsewhere, leaving Peter and me to start shopping for another home.'

During this period of frustrations with *The Mosquito Coast*, Peter Weir went on to make the unusual cop thriller, *Witness* (1985), which starred Harrison Ford as a city cop guarding a young boy who lives in a rural Amish community, who was a witness to a murder in the city.

'I've never had a character like Allie in my films before,' said Weir of the central character in *The Mosquito Coast*, 'that I like and dislike in equal measure. Men like Allie have obviously changed the course of the world's history in certain instances - they've become great statesmen or great dictators. They have a cause, and if people must suffer for that cause, then that must be the price.' It was while working on *Witness* that Weir decided that Ford would be ideal to bring the complex character of Allie Fox to life.

For his part, Harrison Ford felt an immediate connection with the character of Allie Fox. 'I don't have any trouble representing something that I understand, and this is a character that I've never felt any difficulty in understanding. So I didn't think of it as a more difficult job than what I'd done before. On the other hand, I was aware that there was an opportunity here for a more complicated characterisation, and because the character is so verbal and effusive, it goes against the kind of characters for which I'm best known. That was the attraction the part held for me, to do something different.'

Having found the right leading man for the prime role, Peter Weir faced the daunting challenge of finding the right young actor to play the crucial pivotal role of Allie Fox's son, Charlie. 'We were looking for a boy about twelve or thirteen,' said Weir of the casting process. 'Diane Crittenden, the casting director, said "there's a boy on this tape, River Phoenix, he's terrific - only he's fifteen." '

Impressed with the tape, which was a screen test for the role which had been conducted with River Phoenix, Peter Weir was, however, still convinced that at fifteen, he was just too old for the part.

Weir had his eyes on Wil Wheaton instead. Having contested the same role in *Stand By Me* against River Phoenix, Wheaton found himself doing it again - though this time he lost, and there was no secondary role he could fill on this film. 'Maybe he was the better actor,' said Wheaton of Phoenix, 'or maybe we were equal and he matched what they wanted better.'

Despite his worries about Phoenix being too old for the role, Peter Weir found himself returning to the young actor's audition tape again and again. What Weir also found interesting was Phoenix's own unusual family background. He found it intriguing that just like the character of Charlie, Phoenix had spent his childhood travelling in Latin America in the wake of his idealistic parents.

'I finally said to myself,' admitted Weir, 'What the hell does it matter how old he is? He looks like Harrison Ford's son! And I cast him.'

Weir's choice was validated when shooting on the film began and he saw the dailies, indicating that Phoenix had a very special screen presence. 'He has the look of someone who has secrets,' said Weir. 'There's something in him and it goes onto film. The last time I remember seeing it in someone unknown was with Mel Gibson on *Gallipoli* in 1981.'

The rest of the roles were being filled rapidly after the two main parts had been cast. British actress Helen Mirren was cast in the role of Mother, Allie Fox's wife, while the younger of the two Fox brothers was to be played by eleven-year-old Jadrien Steele. Two eight year old fashion models, Hilary and Rebecca Gordon, rounded out the cast as the twin daughters of the Fox family.

During the on-off phase of the production of the film, director Weir and producer Hellman had settled on the ideal location for filming *The Mosquito Coast* - the tiny country of Belize, on the Caribbean Coast of Central America, below the Yucatan Peninsula. The cast and international crew set off to Belize for a rough sixteen-week shooting period. Paul Schrader knew that the production of the film would be difficult. He warned *The Mosquito Coast* author Paul Theroux that 'The hardest films to make are those with scenes on ships, or ones set in the tropics, or ones with a lot of kids in them. This one has all three obstacles.'

'To actually experience the heat, the bugs, the mud and the rain,' said Helen Mirren of the location shooting, 'was a million times better than playing it on a studio back lot with a few palm trees.' However, Weir was intent on treating the exotic location as if it was a backlot, in order to hammer though the tight schedule that the film-makers faced. He let everyone know early on that *The Mosquito Coast* was not going to be 'one of those films on which we're going to spend any amounts of months or years up the river, slowly going crazy. We were going to treat this as if it were a back lot.'

In the film, Allie Fox purchases an abandoned 'town' named Jeronimo, which is actually nothing more than several run-down shacks in an over-grown jungle clearing. On this location the Fox family build their elaborate home, incorporating all that would be expected of a civilised dwelling.

Weir felt it important to film the construction of Jeronimo in sequence, an approach similar to that taken on the barn-building sequence in *Witness*. Weir had three versions of Jeronimo built, each one in a more advanced state of construction than the previous one. 'Everything had to be built,' said Weir, 'in the way that Allie Fox would've done it.' When shooting moved on from one Jeronimo set to another, the construction crew did additional work on the previous set. In this way, with the camera team following the construction crew around in circles, the production team was able to film over

several days what would otherwise have taken many months to complete.

The Mosquito Coast is a dramatically different kind of mainstream American film. Its main character is a brilliant and obsessive madman, a Conradian figure whose journey into the jungle brings with him all the problems that he thinks he's escaping from in the United States. Like Dr Frankenstein, he creates a monster, his ice machine, which turns on its creator, destroying the settlement and poisoning the river. This brilliantly-shot sequence emphasises the links between the devastation wrought by Fox's ice machine and that brought upon Japan by the atomic bomb dropped on Hiroshima - it's no accident that the ice machine is named 'fat boy', an amalgamation of 'little boy' and 'fat man', the names of the bombs dropped on Hiroshima and Nagasaki at the end of World War Two.

The novel of *The Mosquito Coast* is narrated by Charlie Fox, Allie's son, who both adores and resents his father. Some of this is carried over into the

Helen Mirren played River Phoenix's mother in The
Mosquito Coast. She developed a friendship with the boy
and was present at his memorial service.

film with River Phoenix's Charlie occasionally providing narration to the film, but it is the unbearable and unlikeable Allie Fox who dominates proceedings.

It is this that gives the film some of its problems and it certainly turned many of the American film critics against it. The negativity and unlikeability of the Allie Fox character led to much press criticism of the finished film. *The New York Times* commented: 'If the characters in a film wind up alienating the audience as thoroughly as Allie Fox does (despite the canny, snappish performance of Harrison Ford in the role), then the specifics of what happens to them hardly matters at all.'

Vincent Canby, again writing in *The New York Times*, criticised the shifting of the focus of the film away from Charlie's perceptions of his father, to

Charlie (River Phoenix) sets out to sabotage the ice machine to scare the mercenaries in The Mosquito Coast.

the domineering character of Allie Fox himself. 'Without Charlie to inter-
cede, Allie finally becomes something much worse than a relentless, if brilliant, bully. He becomes a monumental bore.' Canby went on to praise
Phoenix in the role of Charlie, the voice who should have been the true focus
of the film: '[River] Phoenix is as good as the screenplay and direction allow
him to be. The problem is not in the performances, but in the way they have
been presented, most of the time in a cool, dispassionate, third-person narrative style, stripped of Charlie's troubled thoughts and feelings that give the
book its emotional force.'

Other writers picked up on the same point as a hook for their criticism.
David Denby in *New York* Magazine said 'In Theroux's 1982 novel, Allie is
seen from the point of view of his older son, thirteen-year-old Charlie, who is
overwhelmed by his dad. It takes a long time for the scales to fall from Charlie's eyes. But in the movie, Charlie is played by the talented River Phoenix
(from *Stand By Me*), a warily intelligent actor of fifteen who looks like he
should catch on quickly enough. Phoenix narrates, which still anchors the
material in Charlie's point-of-view, but as he speaks, the camera impersonal-
ly takes everything in, immediately undermining Charlie's awe. We get
bored waiting for the kid to wise up. His gradual disenchantment is the only
dramatic moment in the film, and it's not nearly enough.'

British critic David Robinson, writing in *The Times*, picked up on
Phoenix's performance in the film as being particularly worthy of praise.
'The insights of child actors are often astonishing: River Phoenix, with a way
of intimating depths of secret anxieties, is every bit the equal of the adult
players.'

Director Peter Weir was quite taken by Phoenix when he started work
shooting on the film: 'He was obviously going to be a movie star,' said Weir
of the young actor, who was now in only his third film role. Due to the logis-
tics of the production, the daily rushes ('dailies') had to be sent out from
Belize to the United States for processing, then back to Belize to be screened
for the director to monitor the progress of the film. There was, therefore, a
delay between the start of shooting and Weir getting to see his first dailies,
the footage that would reassure the director that this huge, risky project was
progressing on the right lines. When the first batch of film came back from
being processed in the United States to the location in Belize, Weir was
pleased to see that Phoenix was coming across extraordinarily well on
screen.

'People who know film - me, Harrison Ford, my wife - could see that
River was something else,' Weir said at the time. 'When a big close up would
come on the screen, it was like when you were a kid and you went to a film
and you couldn't keep your eyes off a character. It's something apart from
the acting ability. Laurence Olivier never had what River had.'

*Director Peter Weir discusses the next scene with River on
The Mosquito Coast location set. Peter Weir was
particularly interested in River's childhood experiences
and how they could inform his portrayal of Charlie in the
film.*

Playing a minor part in the film was actress Martha Plimpton, daughter of actor Keith Carradine. Plimpton had been born and raised in New York City. Martha's mother Shelley Plimpton was also an actress, appearing in the original Broadway cast of *Hair*, as well as in such counterculture cult films as *Putney Swope* (1969) and *Alice's Restaurant* (1969).

At the age of ten, Plimpton was spotted by producer Joseph Papp in a film workshop and he cast her in *The Haggadah*, a play he was involved in at New York's Public Theatre. Plimpton then found a degree of fame and notoriety in a series of Calvin Klein commercials as a tomboy character whose catch phrase was 'I hate competition. I'm a terrible loser.'

The series of advert appearances led to her first feature film role, in Alan J. Pakula's *Rollover* (1981), and eventually she came to be cast by Peter Weir in *The Mosquito Coast*, as the daughter of the preacher, Reverend Spellgood.

River Phoenix and Martha Plimpton had met over a year before they were cast together in *The Mosquito Coast*. 'We couldn't stand each other,' recalled Phoenix of this inauspicious start to what was to be Phoenix's longest lasting romantic relationship. Once shooting started on *The Mosquito Coast*, however, both Phoenix and Plimpton began to see each other differently. 'We realised we'd both changed a lot,' said Phoenix, although he was at a loss to pinpoint exactly what those changes, between the ages of about thirteen and fifteen, were. 'I don't know. We're just cooler, I guess. We both grew a couple of inches!'

The beginning of a serious relationship between Plimpton and Phoenix on *The Mosquito Coast* was to the great pleasure of director Peter Weir, as it confirmed his good judgement in his casting of the film. Weir also felt that the tensions featured in the film between the father and son might also echo some of the tensions felt at home among the Phoenix family, now that River Phoenix was well on his way to being a successful film actor. 'With a young person who suddenly becomes the key breadwinner of a family,' said Weir, 'there's an incredible amount of rearranging of things in the family hierarchy, and sometimes a tension develops, particularly with the father. I don't know if that was true of John [Phoenix]. But River wanted to compensate. He didn't want to spoil the family's closeness.'

John Phoenix was in Belize with his son, as the legally required chaperone, but his father seemed to be uneasy with the filmic role his son was playing in *The Mosquito Coast*. Weir was also aware that the young actor was staging something of a minor food rebellion when his father not around. Instead of following the strict vegan diet laid down by the family, he would eat what were frowned-upon items. 'He'd stuff himself with a Mars Bar and a Coke,' Weir said of Phoenix's secret dietary rebellion. 'It seemed a healthy steam valve,' was Weir's opinion at the time, but this early example of Phoenix's willingness to put aside his principles for pleasure may have been

a major contributing factor to the circumstances surrounding his death in 1993.

   The Phoenix lifestyle and family history were now becoming part of the public relations machine built up by John and Arlyn around Phoenix. Now that he was playing a role which seemed to feature uncanny echoes of his own family's past, that story was being used in the promotion of the film, and of River Phoenix in particular. Previous press releases to accompany his films had Phoenix being raised in Shadow Hills, California, but as soon as it was useful to the family to use their rather more unusual background and Phoenix's upbringing in particular, the story was changed. For *The Mosquito Coast* the River Phoenix weird childhood PR bandwagon went into overdrive. The angle for many of the articles on the film was how closely Phoenix's own background matched that of the character he was playing in the new film.

   Phoenix himself felt closer to the character of Charlie Fox for that very reason. '*The Mosquito Coast* tells you to be true to someone you love. I knew that character so well because I was that character, I knew his whole past.'

River Phoenix with Harrison Ford in The Mosquito Coast.
River got on well with his well-known co-star who
recognised River's intense screen presence.

The implication of this statement from River Phoenix was that his childhood wanderings had left some marks on his character.

Phoenix was delighted to discover that Harrison Ford was one of Hollywood's more down-to-earth star presences. 'He's really great. He wasn't a "movie star", and it was nice to hang out with him. I just can't stand movie stars, the kind who think they're special. We all get up in the morning, go to the bathroom, take a shower, eat breakfast. We're all pretty much the same.'

'River is a natural actor,' said Harrison Ford of his youthful co-star. 'He is inventive, smart and susceptible to all kinds of influences. He is also very serious about his work.'

Phoenix found that playing opposite Ford helped him fine tune his own performance. 'I hate the "actory" way of saying things,' said Phoenix. 'I just try to be in the scene's reality. Sometimes Harrison would say a line with more intensity and my reaction would be different.'

River Phoenix found Harrison Ford to be a positive role model on his own ambitions as an actor and in his approach to Hollywood. Like the Phoenix family, Ford tried to distance himself from Hollywood, only staying in LA when required to be there to work. 'Harrison was down to earth,' said Phoenix. 'I had read that he was cold, but he was actually very warm; it's just that in his position you have so many phoney people trying to dig at you that you've got to have a shield up. He's a very nice man, wise and practical. His ideals are very practical, logical. I learned a lot from him. The biggest thing about Harrison is that he makes acting look so easy, he's so casual and so sturdy. I had a great time [working with him]. We dealt with each other on a very honest level. I understood where he was coming from [in his approach to *The Mosquito Coast*] and I think he understood where I was coming from.'

Seven months in the jungle making *The Mosquito Coast* had also given River Phoenix a more relaxed outlook on life. 'If anything I used to take things too seriously,' Phoenix said of his approach to acting in his early films. 'I learned [on *The Mosquito Coast*] that even among the chaos and discomfort you need to have the freedom of standing back and laughing and not to take it all too seriously. Yet it is a serious job.'

With the dramatic experience of *The Mosquito Coast* behind him, and the maturing influence of a steady relationship with Martha Plimpton, Phoenix now had to find a new direction in his career. He was leaving behind the cute child roles of *Explorers, Stand By Me* and *The Mosquito Coast* with every passing month, as he moved from what had been an eventful childhood into his teenage years. Not ready to play leading man roles in fully 'grown up' films, Phoenix did have one immediate ambition he wanted to tackle, to appear in 'an intelligent teen comedy, if that's possible'.

Chapter 4

GROWING UP on film has never been easy for child actors and actresses. River Phoenix found himself just the latest in a long line of child stars who had to make difficult choices in their late teenage years, hoping to traverse this difficult period to reap the rewards of full adult stardom. Through fear of failure, more than anything else, River Phoenix found himself starring in 1987 in two of the worst movies he was ever to make: *A Night in the Life of Jimmy Reardon* and *Little Nikita*.

Set in 1962, William Richert's *A Night in the Life of Jimmy Reardon* tries very hard to rise a notch above the usual teen comedy. Indeed, all the elements are there - the spoilt rich kids, the graduation ball, the casual sex, the music, the cars and the pretension - but in the hands of writer-director William Richert, the film strives to become something more than the usual run-of-the-mill teen comedy.

The film tells of events over a couple of days in the life of seventeen-year-old Jimmy Reardon, Chicago's very own sixties Casanova who lives with well-to-do self-made parents in Chicago's North Shore. He and his friends have graduated from school and face the difficult choice of which college to attend. Except Jimmy has more problems than the rest - he's already spent his college fund obtaining an abortion for one of his conquests, who may have conned him anyway. His mother Faye (Jane Hallaren) says he'll now have to go to McKinley College, dad's old local Chicago business school, as it's the only way his father (Paul Koslo), who believes in people making their own way in life, will cough up the cash for the fees.

The one girl Jimmy Reardon really wants to be with is Lisa (Meredith Salenger), but her parents don't approve of Jimmy, so she keeps him at a distance. She's heading off to college in Hawaii, so Jimmy concocts a plan to go with her, but he's got to raise the air fare first. The film follows his attempts to raise the money from various friends and acquaintances.

His final night of hell begins when he gives a ride to a friend of his

After The Mosquito Coast River began to break away from his 'child star' image.

mother, Joyce Fickett (Ann Magnuson), only to allow his amorous entanglement with her to delay him in picking up Lisa to go to the graduation ball. Although in the end he fails in his desperate battle to save Lisa from some football jock, the evening's traumas do bring Jimmy and his father to a new rapport and understanding.

'I don't want to look down at that film,' said Phoenix of his first top-billed role: 'It's not at all that I'm too good for it. I did it because I wanted to do something lighter than *Stand By Me* which was very intense. [I was looking for] a vehicle that could take me out of the boy thing. I figured it could help me to grow up. It wasn't meant to be a teenage film.'

Within his own family there was some debate over whether Phoenix should even take the role, due to the sex involved and the apparent advocating of promiscuity on behalf of the Jimmy Reardon character. John Phoenix voted against Phoenix doing the film because of the 'moral problems', but mother Arlyn was more in favour. Director William Richert swung the vote to a yes, according to Phoenix's recollection of the audition for the role. 'When I entered the room, he said " You're Jimmy!" I was really flattered.'

John's reservations about the sex scenes were overcome to the extent that, for the first time, Phoenix did not have either of his parents on the set as

River with Meredith Salenger in A Night in the Life of Jimmy Reardon (1988). It was insecurity that forced Phoenix to take the role and it proved to be one of the worst of his career.

his official chaperone. Instead, this time around the chore fell to his less attentive grandfather 'which wasn't enough to keep me seeing things in perspective. It was weird. I'm glad that somebody from my family is always around. I really grew up on that set. I had my first love scenes; they don't look simulated either, you know, fake, like a lot of grown up ones.'

A Night in the Life of Jimmy Reardon was based on Richert's own autobiographical novel *Aren't You Even Gonna Kiss Me Goodbye?*, written at the age of 19. The gap of some 20 years, however, had changed Richert's own outlook on his novel. 'I did have to imaginatively relocate the kid who wrote the book, and let him write the script. Thus I became father to the kid of twenty years ago. It was an interesting confrontation.'

River Phoenix felt that *Jimmy Reardon* was one teen comedy with an overall message for its prospective audience. 'The message is "slow down and think about what you're doing before you do it. Weigh the pros and cons, what's best for you". Of course, you can get paranoid analysing each situation you're faced with. Sometimes you've got to go with your instinct.'

In taking on the character of Jimmy Reardon, Phoenix was indeed going by his instincts. He needed to find a role to bring him out of the childhood parts he'd been playing, one that would capitalise on his ever growing teen appeal - 'the thinking teen's crumpet' as one British critic put it. This seemed to be the part - what better way to make the break with his previous film characters than by playing a character that confronts head on what all his previous roles had lacked - sex. However, like his father, Phoenix had his reservation about playing this Casanova role.

'I had some moral problems getting behind that film. It's not that those characters don't exist but I'm not sure how valuable that kind of film is. Let's say I took those jobs out of an insecurity, out of a feeling that I might never work again.' Most actors will recognise that feeling of insecurity, the notion that possibly any job is better than no job at all. However, this pair of films (*Jimmy Reardon* and *Little Nikita*) represented the last time Phoenix had to compromise himself - after this he only took roles he really wanted.

'A lot of people entrust themselves to you and look up to you,' said Phoenix, expressing his worries about how his teenage fans might regard his on screen sexual antics. 'I'm speaking about a lot of teenage girls who may see the movie. I'm the monogamous type and I believe romance is important in sex, and *A Night in the Life of Jimmy Reardon* doesn't always present it that way. I could see a stage in my life where I'd be freer with sex - there's nothing wrong with that, but I do believe the circumstance is important in sex and how it's portrayed. Doing it just for the sensation and immediate gratification is selfish. We all have these kinds of urges and feelings inside us and we can't always suppress them. But I'm not against erotic films. *9½ Weeks* and *The Unbearable Lightness of Being* are great - they're a different ball game.'

There were differences between the character of Jimmy Reardon as initially perceived by Richert and the character who ended up on screen. Originally, Reardon was conceived of as a poet whose love for women matched his despair and poverty. Somewhere along the line this angle got lost, and the on screen character of Reardon comes across as an unsympathetic, unfeeling character who deserves all his misfortunes. Indeed, Phoenix worried that he was not the right actor to carry off the role successfully. 'It should have starred someone a bit more masculine, like Tom Cruise.'

Despite his 'moral problems' with the film's portrayal of sex, Phoenix had few problems when it actually came down to acting out the sex scenes, including one with the Joyce Fickett character (Ann Magnuson), a friend of Reardon's mother and object of his film father's secret affections.

'I didn't even think of it,' said Phoenix of tackling these scenes. 'If I can give myself credit in acting, it's that I can lose myself easily, forgetting about the camera. Subconsciously, you always know it's there and sometimes your

River in compromising position with co-star Ann Magnuson in A Night In The Life of Jimmy Reardon. River's father was anxious about the morality of the part.

*River Phoenix as the teenage Casanova, Jimmy Reardon.
He said that he did not really feel macho
enough for the part.*

ego wants to act a certain way but you can't think "What will Tom think if he sees this movie? Will he think I'm cool in this scene if I do this?"'

'In *A Night in the Life of Jimmy Reardon*,' continued Phoenix, 'I'm sure I did some posing here and there, but that was part of the character, too. It called for that. I was thinking from Jimmy's perspective, and it was quite exciting and very entertaining. I mean, watching rushes was another thing altogether - or seeing the movie, forget it! I feel self-conscious, like it's not me.'

The film had an interesting score, with occasional contemporary pop songs thrown in and a fairly unusual modern jazz-based score to accompany the climatic car chase sequence. But also, in an interesting development, River Phoenix actually wrote the theme song. While acting paid the rent, music continued to be a significant sideline. Phoenix had maintained his interest in music from his childhood: 'Music is a hobby, because I'm not making any money out of it, but I put just as much conviction into that as I do into my acting.' It also opened up the possibility of other creative avenues. Phoenix said: 'I wrote the theme tune to Jimmy Reardon, and the director told me that if there is a video made, then I could co-direct it. Sometimes I think I'd like to be a director.'

In *The Mosquito Coast*, Phoenix had experienced little difficulty getting into the mind of the character of Charlie Fox as the storyline of the film and background of the character bore enough similarities with elements of Phoenix's own background. As the character of Jimmy Reardon was so far removed from his own experiences, Phoenix had more work than usual to do in realising the part. 'Becoming a character is a slow process. I start off just by stripping myself from who I am, by neutralising myself, and then I fantasise about what the character would do and play a lot of mind games.'

Critical reaction to the film was predictably poor, with Britain's film journal of record, *The Monthly Film Bulletin*, claiming that the casting of Phoenix in the central role adds to the film's failures: 'The problems are compounded by the casting of River Phoenix, whose air and appearance of being closer to twelve than seventeen makes, for example, Jimmy's aspirations towards beatnik poetry ("I have come back from a pit of pimps and whores") more than a little unconvincing.' Conversely, other critics felt that Phoenix was the only notable element of the entire package, with Shaun Usher in Britain's *Daily Mail* writing 'Phoenix is excellent and teenagers especially will relish the deadpan confessions of a Casanova more familiar with seduction than with shaving.'

Perhaps the strongest praise came from Roger Kean in *Movie* Magazine, who wrote 'River Phoenix is marvellous as the generally unlikeable Reardon.' Kean went on to highlight the comparisons that the promotion of the

film was attempting to draw between Phoenix and James Dean, prophetically writing: 'He's been likened to James Dean - the looks, possibly the level of success in so few, but major films. Dean killed himself at 28. Is that to be the hot-house end for River Phoenix?'

In the meantime, the young actor continued to pursue his teen idol status, playing up to the female teenage fan following that had developed, turning Phoenix into a worldwide cover star and pinup. Second billed after Sidney Poitier in Richard Benjamin's 1987 film *Little Nikita*, River Phoenix plays Jeffrey Nicholas Grant, who, as *Little Nikita*'s advertising copy had it: '...went to bed an all-American kid and woke up the son of Russian spies!'

From Phoenix's entrance under the opening titles, *Little Nikita* looks for all the world like just another teen film. He is the 'all-American' kid, goofing off, crashing his bike, dressing up for his girlfriend and harbouring dreams of joining the air force academy as a cadet.

However, this film doesn't know where it is going or what it is trying to be, getting muddled from the start when it tries to lay thriller and cold-war espionage plots over the teen hero focus. A rogue Russian agent, named Scuba because of his love of water, is killing off other agents in an attempt to blackmail his Russian handlers into handing over $200,000. His targets are 'sleepers', agents planted in America in the late sixties, under directions to live American lives and have American families, awaiting the day when they will be reawakened and sent back into the field to fight the good fight for Communism.

The cold war rhetoric of *Little Nikita* has dated very rapidly from its 1988 release. Despite the fact that the Russian diplomats fear coming to the attention of the media, whereas older agent Konstantin Karpov used to fear the CIA, nothing, as Karpov states, has changed that much in the war between the superpowers.

Into all this comes Sidney Poitier, an experienced FBI agent whose partner was killed by the very same Soviet agent named Scuba, 20 years previously. Alerted to Scuba's renewed activity and the presence of old-time Russian agent Karpov, Poitier's Roy Parmenter begins investigating.

Coming across Jeff Grant due to his air force application, Parmenter discovers that his parents are using assumed names. Richard and Elizabeth Grant are not who they claim to be, as the real Richard and Elizabeth Grant died in 1891. Poitier's character is the kind of detective who spends much of his time sitting at his desk, looking moody and talking to himself in order to work out the plot and explain it to an increasingly bemused audience. Emphasising the incestuous nature of the characters, Parmenter also begins an affair with a guidance counsellor at Jeff Grant's school, after moving into the neighbourhood to spy on his parents.

Parmenter bluntly breaks the news of his parents' origins to Jeff, who

then finds himself threatened by Karpov, so his re-activated Soviet agent parents will set up a cash hand over to trap Scuba. This all builds to a strangely unexciting climax, with chases across a pier and on a trolley bus heading for the Mexican border, before the inevitable happy ever after climax. Hey - Jeff's parents may be Russian spies, but they love him, after all!

Richard Benjamin had been impressed by Phoenix's body of work and felt he was the right actor, again with the right family background to bring out the confusion that Jeff Grant faces when his world changes around him. 'They are talented kids,' said Richard Benjamin of the Phoenix clan. 'And their parents have instilled in them a sense of morality.' But in too many scenes, Phoenix seems unsure at what level of emotional intensity he should pitch it. He is constantly on the move: running, jumping, pacing, and never talks quietly when shouting will do. His character has a girlfriend (Lucy Deakins) who we see very little of, and we hear a bit about a school he never seems to go to. He's also got a group of friends who vanish after they've served their purpose in the introductory scenes.

The father-son relationship Phoenix explores in this film is not between him and his parents, but with the outsider, Sidney Poitier. In the air force academy interview, Parmenter tells Jeff simply to be himself, but the script has Phoenix upping the adolescent angst by replying: 'I don't know what myself is.' There are serious issues the film could have explored more here, but instead it's all thrown away on feeble light hearted comic relief scenes, which simply do not gel with the thriller-spy plot that runs alongside them. Throw in some positively childish teen romance scenes, and you've got a film that's as confused as the central character is.

Little Nikita's major problem is the script. With at least four credited writers having a hand in the story and screenplay, it is no wonder the film is packed with ridiculous lines and situations, which the cast do their best to carry off with some semblance of a straight face. Phoenix himself had grave reservations about the film: 'The biggest difficulty was selling myself the whole plot. Being the son of Russian spies is far-fetched for me, but that's because I'm me. It was hard to adjust to that.'

Phoenix faced an insurmountable acting challenge with the character of Jeff Grant, who suddenly has to deal with the fact that his parents are strangers. With another script and another director, perhaps Phoenix could have made something spectacular of the role. As it stands, it's a very disappointing piece of work from an actor who at this stage in his career was trying to live up to the past promise he'd shown.

'Another challenge was the transition the character has to make from being a kid with a really decent life, a kid who feels very secure and dreams of becoming an air force pilot, into someone who has the rug pulled right out from under him,' complained Phoenix. 'I had to evolve from a real happy-

Little Nikita: veteran actor Sidney Poitier as an FBI agent, comforting the distraught Jeff Grant (River Phoenix) when he discovers his parents are Russian agents.

go-lucky guy into someone who's torn between his loyalty to his family, his conscience and his duty to his country.'

Like most of his films, Phoenix nevertheless seems to have regarded *Little Nikita* as a learning experience. He felt that perhaps the role was beyond him, but had tried to make something of it. 'It was a challenging role and I don't know if I completely succeeded.'

Of course, given River Phoenix's political views, he had various problems with the representation of some characters in *Little Nikita*, too.

'I really didn't like the way the Russians were portrayed - it was a bit stereotypical,' he said. 'At the end, when Richard Bradford [as KGB agent Karpov] says "You know, Russians don't shoot their children," I felt it was a bit too easy, an attempt to compensate for his previous ruthlessness. But it's hard to be objective about it. I think it's a solid film.'

On his learning curve, Phoenix probably had the most to gain from working with his co-star Sidney Poitier. Poitier's multi-faceted career as a performer, writer and director has spanned four decades, and brought him the 1992 Lifetime Achievement Award from the American Film Institute.

Throughout the sixties Poitier found himself one of America's most popular film actors, winning praise for roles in films which often dealt with difficult themes of race, such as *To Sir With Love* (1967), *In the Heat of the Night* (1967) and *Guess Who's Coming To Dinner?* (1967) In the 1970s he began his second career as a director, at first starring in the films he directed. After ten years off the screen, Poitier returned to acting in 1987-88 with roles in the adventure film *Shoot To Kill* with Tom Berenger and Kirstie Alley, and *Little Nikita*.

'I was so open to his advice and suggestions,' Phoenix said of his working relationship with Sidney Poitier. 'He's a wonderful person and a really bright man, who gave me tips about life too, not just acting. He's very open minded and still a curious man, who's not afraid of learning. So many people make everything concrete, especially when they get older.'

Little Nikita was not a success, either financially at the box office, critically or simply as a decent film. *Variety* criticised it, saying: '*Little Nikita* never really materialises as a taut espionage thriller and winds up as an unsatisfying execution of a clever premise...' But the newspaper did add that Poitier '...seems just right for the role. Poitier begins an investigation that leads to an almost avuncular bonding with Phoenix.'

Although both *A Night in the Life of Jimmy Reardon* and *Little Nikita* fail in their own right as entertaining films, both propelled River Phoenix onto the covers and into the profile pages of teen magazines around the world. He became the 'green' lobby's pin-up figure, with a cover appearance on a vegetarian magazine.

Phoenix could have fulfilled the promise of his earlier career in the character of Jeff Grant in Little Nikita but a poor script and inadequate director let him down.

All this exposure provided a platform for River Phoenix to pass off his opinion on any subject under the sun, from the global environment to politics, to fashion. Many of the statements sounded as if they were coming from a teenage sage or oracle, and some returned again and again to haunt an older and less pretentious River Phoenix. 'What I'm really concerned with is the air, the water, the earth that we live on,' he said. 'It's bad enough and, at this rate, poetry won't last, good movies won't last.'

One of the press junkets that was prepared to promote the Phoenix image saw the actor come out with this: 'I'm quite in love with the human race and this planet that we live on and I see life as fresh and beautiful, not because I have the world in my hands, but because it's just my reality.' It was a line that was to be repeated to him many times, such that it became something of an embarrassment. And when he spoke of 'pure and clean living' the media were only too ready to throw it back at him after his drug-induced death.

'I also get very frustrated with the pace of life and the way the world goes,' he once said. 'I want so badly for people to communicate with each other. With all this technology is this the best we can do? It's depressing. But there's also an optimistic side of me that believes that we live in an incredible time and that if we all come together on the important issues we could really accomplish a lot.'

Phoenix had his own particular area in which he hoped one day to make a personal intervention. 'One thing I would like to do when I have the money is buy thousands of acres in the Brazilian rain forest and make a national park, so no one can bulldoze it to put a MacDonald's there.'

With his fee per film starting at $350,000 as from *Running On Empty*, Phoenix could afford to go someway towards that ambition shortly before his death. 'I've just bought 800 acres of forest on the border of Panama and Costa Rica. [I want to] buy the last "first growth forest" and turn it into a national park. It's a human tragedy of immense proportions. Many native Indians in that region are losing their homes daily, and it's going to affect both you and me, because that's where most of the world's oxygen comes from. The Amazon rain forests are the world's lungs and without them we will not be able to breath. It's a very scary thought and it's not too far off.'

Phoenix also had the chance, through the teen magazine profiles, to expound on behalf of groups he supported, like People For Ethical Treatment of Animals (PETA): 'One of my beliefs is about harmlessness to animals. I don't believe in eating meat or using any animal by-products or contributing to suppressing animals.'

However, the whole teen idol promotion involved Phoenix getting sucked into a lot of processes that he despised, such as glamorous photo shoots, repetitive press interviews and answering questions from gushing

Male bonding: - River Phoenix and Sidney Poitier have a game of basketball in Little Nikita, another film which explored an unconventional 'father-son' relationship.

*The perils of being a teenage idol: River Phoenix
posing for a fashion shot.*

thirteen and fourteen year olds. Of one fashion photo shoot he complained: 'I was dressed up like a model, told to pose in certain ways, to tilt my head, push my lips out, suck in my cheeks. And I'd be tired at the end of the day so I'd just give the damned photographer what he wanted. It was the most mortifying experience. And the photographs were the ugliest, the most contrived. It wasn't me.'

Phoenix was aware of the needs of the publicity machine and the fact that creating and promoting an image was a necessary component of his career ('...it helps as far as your rating in Hollywood is concerned...'), but he was to become increasingly unhappy with the image he was now creating as the years went on. At the time it was the process itself which irked him: 'Sometimes I have to be a salesman and do interviews and promote my film, but I don't get involved with all the publicity stuff as far as trying to promote my own image and trying to make it into something. People are constantly trying to make an image for you. They'll dress you up and tell you to pose in a certain way and take all these pictures. And you'll see all these pictures in magazines everywhere and it's kinda embarrassing because it's not you.'

Phoenix tried to deal with the image problem and the fact that many actors come to believe in their image more than their real selves by trying to separate out Hollywood and film making from the real business of life. 'I've kept my ego and my happiness completely separate from my work. I don't depend on my work to make me feel good about myself. In fact, if I see my face on the cover of a magazine I go into remission. I shut myself out and freak. I don't like being out there.'

Often these interviews would end with questions concerning Phoenix's ambitions - not so much in film and acting, but in his personal life. Was the teen heart throb ever going to settle down and get married? Did he want kids? It gave Phoenix a chance to gaze into the future, to try and figure out what it actually was that he wanted from his life. 'I want kids, a family of my own. I'd like to give them the first eight years of their lives in the country. Then I'd want them educated, which I wasn't formally, although I had a tutor once when I was twelve . At times I miss a formal education, but at others I thank God for everything else I have now. What I have got from my childhood aren't toys, but memories. And happy memories are better than any toy.'

With both his teen starring roles in *A Night in the Life of Jimmy Reardon* and *Little Nikita*, River Phoenix had tried to move beyond his eldest child roles into leading man roles in teen comedies. From their respective failures, he'd learned his lessons, and for his next film, *Running On Empty*, he'd return to the family structure movie, and gain an Oscar nomination in the process.

Chapter 5

FROM HIS misadventures in the world of teen comedies, River Phoenix went on to make two very different film appearances, one of which was to earn him great critical acclaim and an Oscar nomination for Best Supporting Actor. The other saw him appear, albeit briefly, in one of the year's biggest blockbuster movies, a career move that did the young actor's visibility no harm whatsoever.

The first of these two films was *Running On Empty*, the tale of the Pope family - mum, dad and two brothers - on the run for fifteen years, moving from town to town, to evade the attentions of the FBI. The children are suffering because of the activities of the parents. In the sixties Arthur and Annie Pope were college based political activists, who with a group of friends bombed a Government-funded napalm factory. Unintentionally, the attack critically injured a janitor who was inside the building. The Popes found themselves on the FBI's Ten Most Wanted list and their flight began. Taking their two-year old son Danny (River Phoenix), they head off, attempting for fifteen years to forge a 'normal' family life despite being forced to relocate frequently.

The film opens with Danny now seventeen and the family facing the prospect of having to move on once more. Danny's brother (Jonas Abry) is too young yet to appreciate the wrench of leaving people behind every time the family moves on, but Danny has formed attachments, primarily with Lorna Phillips, once again played by Martha Plimpton, the daughter of the music teacher who is trying to encourage Danny to develop his musical talents. Danny wants to stop running and build a life for himself. Can the Pope family stand such a division?

'People think the Popes are like my family, but they aren't,' objected Phoenix when the similarities were pointed out. 'My parents were never on the run. We moved because we couldn't pay the rent or something. My parents would sympathise with the Popes, but they are pacifists. My mother

No longer a child star with a cute baby face, during 1988 River began to assert his independence both as an actor and as a person.

would never throw a bomb, it's just not in her nature. Also my family is bru-
tally honest with each other. We don't hide our feelings the way the Popes
did. And I don't think letting go would ever hurt my family. It's the other
way around really. We've never had this kind of stable family life before and
I'm enjoying it. I like coming home and having members of my family
around.'

Phoenix believed that unlike the family in *Running On Empty*, the experiences of his parents and young family as they moved around the Americas
were beneficial. 'My parents kept on moving like the family in the film, but
without having to change their name at each stop. They learnt a lot from
their experience, so they didn't feel cheated or bitter.' (Phoenix had apparently forgotten that changing the family name was exactly what John
Phoenix did do on their return to the United States in 1977.)

Some aspects of the family in Running on Empty bore an
uncanny resemblance to Phoenix's own peripatetic upbringing. Left
to right: River Phoenix, Christine Lahti and Jonas Abry on the run.

The on-the-run parents in *Running On Empty* are played by Judd Hirsch and Christine Lahti. Lahti recognised something of herself in the character of Annie Pope, as she was herself involved in non-violent protest in the sixties. Behind the camera on *Running On Empty* was director Sidney Lumet, one of America's most successful and respected film directors who started his career, like River Phoenix, as a child actor in 1939, aged fifteen. His film directorial debut was *Twelve Angry Men* (1957), the courtroom drama that was set within the jury room and starred Henry Fonda. The film was nominated for three Academy Awards, including Best Picture, but it was *Network* (1976), a biting satire on the growing power of television personalities which won four Oscars, including Best Actor posthumously for Peter Finch.

Lumet's films have often dealt with controversial or counter-culture issues, so *Running On Empty* was ideal material for him to tackle, almost a variation on his immediately preceding film *Daniel* (1983). That controversial film was his version of the E.L. Doctorow novel *The Book Of Daniel*, which is about the lives of two children who must confront their backgrounds in order to deal with their own lives in protest-filled 1960s America. *Daniel* was withdrawn from American cinemas within days of its release.

'Just as it was released that Korean airliner was shot down,' explained Lumet. 'People didn't want to see a movie about "Commies". It wasn't about politics, it was about how something means more to people than their children. It could have been about stockbrokers or workaholics. *Running On Empty* was the same subject, exactly. But it had a more optimistic ending.'

Lumet considered *Running On Empty* a 'hard film to classify. It's not exactly a coming-of-age story. Danny, the older son, is already mature and knowledgeable. It's more about the consequences of our actions and the dynamics of what makes a family. These people's lives are a mess. The children are the only success they've got. The film is about their inability to break up this family.'

Screenwriter and co-executive producer Naomi Foner agreed: 'That's really what I was trying to write about - the story of what happens to every family when parents have to let their child go. Parenting is the only love story that, to end successfully, means the participants must ultimately leave each other.'

Foner was pleased by the casting of River Phoenix in the pivotal role of seventeen-year-old Danny Pope, the aspiring pianist who doesn't want to run any more. She was, however, shocked by Phoenix's lack of education and bought him a collection of literary novels for his eighteenth birthday in an effort to expand the young actor's mind. 'He was totally, totally without education. I mean, he could read and write, and he had an appetite for it, but he had no deep roots into any kind of sense of history or literature.'

However, Foner saw this lack of formal training and education as an undoubted advantage in his acting: 'Some of the reason that he was so talented was that stuff didn't get processed through his head or through some preconception of what it was supposed to be.'

Christine Lahti, his on-screen mother, was worried about acting opposite the rising star with no formal dramatic training. 'I was wary of working with River. Not only because he is so young, but also because he's had no training. But he's really good, very honest; you can't ask for more from another actor.'

She did have her problems with the diet conscious actor, though. 'I drank a Diet Coke on the set of *Running On Empty*, and he was furious with me. He was so adamant about clean, pure living.'

Director Sidney Lumet was aware of Phoenix's lack of formal training and was willing to use that in the film to reach for the truth at the heart of the character of the confused seventeen-year-old facing difficult decisions in his life.

'He's a superb actor with a real technique, despite his years. He's never studied formally, but boy, does he know how to reach inside himself. He's extremely mature for someone his age. I don't know what combination of things make a star. You have to have a very strong clear persona and you have to be a very good actor. He is both, so he ought to have a brilliant career.'

Screenwriter Foner was aware of the echoes that *Running On Empty* had for the Phoenix family, both in the past and at that moment in time. River Phoenix was beginning to strike out more on his own, asserting his independence from the tight knit family unit and from the management of his career by his mother. Foner called Arlyn Phoenix 'a very warm, bright, outgoing woman,' who was only too aware of the relevance of the final scenes of *Running On Empty* for her own relationship with her talented son. 'She knew that one day she would have to say good-bye to him. I think she was saying he was ready to move on.'

River Phoenix himself was forced by the issues in the film to confront the prospect that soon he would be 'leaving' his own parents. 'That is hypothetical still. I have thought about it, and it would be painful for them. But being the kind of parents they are, they would let me go. They have always encouraged me to follow my own instincts.'

Compared to Phoenix's previous film, *Little Nikita*, which has a few surface and thematic connections with the later film, *Running On Empty* is a classy production in which not a frame of film is wasted in telling the anguished story of the turbulent lives of the Popes. The back story of the parents is quickly set up in the beginning, as the two brothers discuss their parents' history over a pile of newspaper clippings, as the family go on the run once again, adopting new identities in a new town.

The desire to develop Danny's musical talents creates the crisis within the Pope family in Running On Empty. River Phoenix had himself had practically no formal education.

The ritual which the Popes undergo every time they move itself reflects the life and techniques an actor must employ. For every new film part River Phoenix had to adopt a new persona, get inside someone else's head. Significantly, he admitted that he sometimes found it difficult to lose elements of the characters he'd adopted after he finished making a film.

'You can't just wake up next morning and be the character,' he said. 'It's a slow process. You have to neutralise yourself before you can become another character. I become non-opinionated, refusing to think from River's perspective and then, slowly, I add characteristics, and start thinking the way the character would.'

In many ways Danny Pope is another in the long line of Phoenix's awkward teenage outsiders. Upon first arriving at the music class, Danny makes

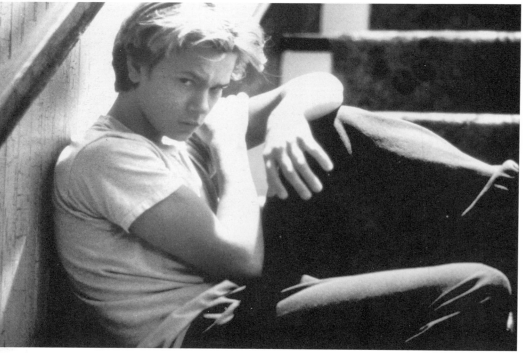

half-hearted attempts to join in the class fun as the tutor explains the rhythmic and structural differences between a Madonna track and Beethoven. He transmits a constant feeling of unease as the family settle into their new surroundings, because he knows that as he's getting older he's changing and new priorities are establishing themselves within him. He has to face the prospect of taking up a college place and carving out a life for himself, no longer being solely defined by his on-the-run family. His fear at separating

The character of Danny Pope in Running On Empty is another in the long line of River's awkward teenage outsiders, only this time it was convincing enough to earn him an Oscar nomination.

from the family is greater than that for any normal teenager, because Danny can't be sure that his parents will continue their flight from the FBI without him as a motivation.

Unlike *Little Nikita*, which failed dismally on both counts and featured an unfocused performance from Phoenix, *Running On Empty* succeeded on almost every level. The physical exuberance which Phoenix displayed in *Little Nikita* but which seemed to have no justification, is here tied to emotional highs and lows, is used sparingly and appropriately. Watching the two films back-to-back it is clear the difference that a good script and a good director could make to a performance from River Phoenix. In *The Mosquito Coast, Running On Empty, Dogfight* and *My Own Private Idaho*, Phoenix is given strong direction, which also motivates him to a better performance and to

contribute in a more concrete way to the success or failure of each individual film, even changing dialogue and staging in *My Own Private Idaho*, for example.

Unlike *Little Nikita*, the teen romance is developed fully as a major plank of the plot in *Running On Empty*. The chemistry between Martha Plimpton and River Phoenix is clear on screen, and their developing romance is the key that unravels the Pope family unit. Their off-screen relationship had con-

River Phoenix with Martha Plimpton, his on- and off-screen girlfriend in Running On Empty. Their mutual attraction was clear and their relationship a crucial dynamic to the film.

His relationship with Martha Plimpton was River's longest lasting; the shooting of Running On Empty gave them uninterrupted time together.

tinued since *The Mosquito Coast*, under the watchful eyes of Phoenix's parents. It was difficult, given both young actors' filmmaking commitments, for them to see each other as often as they would have liked. Working together on *Running On Empty* provided an opportunity for a few months together and their personal intimacy enabled them to act un-selfconsciously on screen.

Running On Empty even features that teen movie cliché, the aspiring Romeo climbing the tree outside a reluctant Juliet's bedroom window. However, the film uses this to lead into a pivotal confession scene where Phoenix as Danny tearfully explains his mysterious background to Plimpton's Lorna Phillips, because he doesn't want to get deeply involved with her while living a lie. Phoenix uses this key moment to lay bare the confusion of the character of Danny Pope as he tries to meet the demands and needs of his parents and the family, while dealing with his own developing needs: 'I don't know what I'm doing!'

Much of the film explores the differing relationships between children and their parents. Like Phoenix's own family, the Popes are a very close family, as clearly demonstrated at the birthday party scene for Lahti's Annie Pope. They quickly welcome Lorna as one of them and clearly display the love and affection they have for each other.

Lorna's own parents are a different matter. We only ever see her father, music teacher Mr Phillips, who seems more interested in developing Danny's musical talents than in his own daughter. Lorna has an older sister who followed through on the musical ambitions which her father had for his offspring, while Lorna is more of an outspoken individualist, who tries to insist that her father knock before entering her room and who resents the stuffy formal Chamber Music recitals he holds.

Phoenix's Danny keeps a newspaper cutting containing photographs of his grandparents, and while attending a music audition for entry to the Juilliard School of Music, a clue leads him to track down his maternal grandmother. The confrontation is confusing for Danny, who poses as a pizza delivery boy and doesn't reveal his own identity; he does nothing to follow up on the meeting. Finding grandparents would be too much like having family roots, too much like having a stable background, which Danny can't afford if the family are to continue moving on.

While family life for Phoenix had been different in tone to that portrayed in *Running On Empty*, the resonances in the film cannot have been lost on him. 'My life certainly hasn't been ordinary: different is the word. It hasn't always been stable - except in the important things which are love and security within the family. Whenever there were strains at home, we could always communicate. The rule was that the younger you were, the louder you were allowed to scream. As the eldest, I just talked.'

Sidney Lumet, the distinguished director of
Running On Empty, built on the understated naturalism
of River's screen technique.

Sidney Lumet recognised this extraordinary ability in the young actor when he was casting the part of Danny Pope. Locking onto the talented young man with the unusual upbringing was ideal for the film. 'He couldn't be ordinary if he tried,' said Lumet of Phoenix. 'As in the film he is seventeen [he turned eighteen during shooting] and he'll want to take off and then there will be the letting go - but letting go with love. Unlike most, there will be a happy ending with his family.' Lumet was of course proved tragically wrong.

Lumet found himself willing to be guided as to the veracity of the material in the film: the feelings and emotions, taking Phoenix's past experiences of life on the road as a useful research tool. 'River doesn't have a false bone in his body. He can't utter a false line. He stopped in the middle of one scene while we were shooting and said 'This feels fake to me'. I listened again. He was right. I cut the scene. So long as River follows his instincts, takes stuff he believes in, there'll be no stopping him. I first saw him in *Stand By Me* and there was such an extraordinary purity about him. Then he did *The Mosquito Coast* and you felt the growth of his understated power.'

Lumet believed that the relationship between the parents and the children in *Running On Empty* was similar to that between River Phoenix and his own parents. 'You never get the sense of driving ambition or calculation among River's family. I think that show business was an accidental solution to a number of financial problems. Quite clearly, if River didn't want to do it or couldn't handle it, he wouldn't. The first thing that matters to his mother is those kids.'

Foreshadowing what was soon to become a problem for River Phoenix, as a very experienced Hollywood director, Sidney Lumet also commented on drugs in the studios at the time he was making *Running On Empty*. 'Drugs are so pervasive now, there's no way to safeguard kids from them. When I speak to a young actor, I just tell him or her at the start of the picture that if anything goes on I'll fire him on the spot. I'll reshoot the entire film if I have to. Aside from my moral detestation, when actors are acting under the influence of drugs, the performance may be going on in their heads, but it isn't happening on the screen.'

Running On Empty garnered a number of award nominations, with Christine Lahti winning the Los Angeles Film Critics' award as Best Actress for her role in the film. River Phoenix was nominated for a Best Supporting Actor Oscar. He was up against some very experienced competition for the award. Also nominated was veteran actor Alec Guiness for his role in the British-made Dickens adaptation *Little Dorrit*; Kevin Kline for his manic comic turn in the British farce *A Fish Called Wanda*; Martin Landau for Francis Ford Coppola's underrated drama *Tucker: The Man and His Dreams*; and one time child actor Dean Stockwell, who secured a nomination for the

Jonathan Demme-directed Mafia comedy-drama *Married to the Mob*.

Phoenix attended the 61st Oscar ceremony on 29th March 1989, dressed in a tuxedo and with Martha Plimpton on his arm. His mother Arlyn Phoenix was also in attendance. Speaking of his nomination, Phoenix hoped the recognition would spur him onto higher things. 'I think that in a way I'm being challenged,' he said. 'I feel that there are great minds up there who would like to see what I can do with an Oscar nomination. I guess many people would change after a nomination in the way they see things. In my case it's really irrelevant in terms of what I do. Still, it was an incredible experience which I will put in my memories, like everything else.'

In the event, Phoenix was not to win the Oscar. It went instead to Kevin Kline, whom Phoenix was soon to star opposite in *I Love You To Death*. However, most critics at the time reckoned that his nomination at such a young age and after only a handful of movies was an indication that he was a talent to watch. It was only a matter of time before River Phoenix would win the golden statuette, they speculated, and it wouldn't be for a supporting role, either, but as Best Actor.

Phoenix was happy to be famous, though. It enabled him to speak out about his environmental pre-occupations and for people to listen to him, if not yet take him seriously. 'If I have some celebrity, I hope I can use it to make a difference. The true social reward is that I can speak my mind and share my thoughts about the environment and civilisation itself. There's so much shit happening with people who are exploiting their positions and creating a lot of negativity.'

After the emotional rigours of *Running On Empty*, Phoenix was looking for something a bit less draining of his acting energies, while capitalising on his success with the honour of the Oscar nomination. The result was his appearance in *Indiana Jones and the Last Crusade* (1988), one of the biggest blockbuster films of all time.

'I wanted to do something light, pure entertainment,' said Phoenix. 'I love the Indiana Jones films and being part of one was a lot of fun for me.'

Although a small part, River Phoenix is the focus of attention as the film opens. He plays the young Indiana Jones, heroic adventuring archaeologist played by Harrison Ford in two previous films. The third instalment in the series opens in Utah, 1912 , with the young Indy on the trail with a scout troop. Exploring some caves, he comes across a group of mercenaries, digging up a cross which once belonged to Cortez in 1520. Determined that the artefact should be in a museum, young Indy launches on a reckless mini-crusade to retrieve the artefact and get it to the correct authorities for safe keeping.

The ten minute sequence is a tour-de-force of physical skill, as well as a

River Phoenix as the young Indiana Jones has his first encounter with a snake, in Indiana Jones and The Last Crusade.

wonderfully humorous re-introduction to the character of Indiana Jones, who had last been on the screen in 1984 in *Indiana Jones and the Temple of Doom*. The opening sequence of the third film recreates many elements from the first *Raiders of the Lost Ark* (1981) to explain how the Indiana Jones character developed many of his trademark characteristics, phobias and even his distinctive way of dressing.

The sequence is basically a chase as Phoenix's young Indy heads off on foot with the cross, pursued by the bad guys. Within seconds the chase has changed to Indy on horseback and his foes following in cars. That leads on to a sequence along the top of a fast-moving circus train, packed with animals and circus gimmicks. Falling into a snake pit gives Indy his phobia for reptiles, while an encounter with an angry rhino leads on to a drop-in visit to a lion. It's here, to the rising Indiana Jones theme music, that Indy obtains his trademark whip, as well as the scar on his chin (which actually belongs to actor Harrison Ford, rather than the character of Indiana Jones).

After escaping the clutches of his pursuers with a magic touch, Indy returns home to Dad (Sean Connery, in off screen voice over only at this stage). Before he can show his father his find, the local sheriff arrives and confiscates the cross, only to return it to the desecrators who Indy had witnessed digging it up. Impressed by young Indy's bravery, the leader of the mercenaries puts his hat on Indy's head. A quick cut, and it's Harrison Ford under the very same hat, battling the very same crooked archaeologist for possession of the very same Cortez Cross, this time on a ship off the Portuguese Coast in 1938. The more mature Indiana Jones swings straight into an action sequence, retrieving the cross once and for all, as the boat explodes, lighting up the night sky.

This entire opening sequence adds up to 20 minutes of film time, and the real story of *Indiana Jones and the Last Crusade* hasn't got going yet. Jones is hired by Julian Glover's philanthropist to follow some clues to find the Holy Grail, the cup Christ drank from during the last supper, which is reputed to contain the secret of immortality. Along the way in this rip-roaring adventure which deliberately pays homage to the old thirties adventure serials, Jones comes across old friends and enemies, including a reunion with his father, Sean Connery, who is teamed up with Harrison Ford to great effect. A superior film to the second Indiana Jones outing, *The Last Crusade* was a world-wide blockbuster, and did River Phoenix's reputation no harm whatsoever.

Phoenix was keen on the action man persona that playing Indiana Jones allowed him to develop. 'It's all non-stop action: running and jumping, twisting and turning, fumbling, finding, keeping, saving from bad guys - that kind of stuff. It's a small part - only ten minutes at the movies beginning, but I really enjoyed it.'

*Playing the young Indy gave River a chance to try
his hand at stunt work.*

Playing the part in *Indiana Jones and the Last Crusade* did not mean a large commitment of time for the young actor in a hurry, but it did mean a large impact was assured. The film also gave Phoenix the chance to try things which his previous film roles had not allowed for - like stunt work. 'I did a lot of the stunts because I felt so much of the character and what he had to do was physical. It would have been lying to have someone else do the stunts. I had the opportunity. It's exciting to see how a dramatic and dangerous situation unfolds - it's fun to witness it in a movie theatre and it's fun to make.'

Although Harrison Ford was the star of the movie, River Phoenix didn't actually get the chance to act opposite him. However, in playing a younger version of the character Harrison Ford had done so much to create, Phoenix looked to the older, more experienced actor for some clues.

'I would just look at Harrison: he would do stuff and I would not mimic it, but interpret it younger,' said Phoenix, explaining his interpretation of the young Indiana Jones. 'Mimicking is a terrible mistake that many people do when they play someone younger, or with an age difference. Mimicking doesn't interpret true because you can't just edit it around.'

Like *Running On Empty, Indiana Jones and the Last Crusade* deals with family relationships under its brash action-adventure surface. The conclusion of the opening sequence featuring Phoenix establishes the relationship between Indiana Jones and his father, Henry Jones. Later in the film, Harrison Ford reunites with his father, played by Sean Connery, and the two play an almost comic double act throughout the movie. As producer Robert Watts said of the films family theme: 'With the River Phoenix as Young Indy scene and the introduction of Sean Connery as Indy's father, we're dealing with personal relationships more in this film then we've ever done before.'

Indiana Jones and the Last Crusade was one of the biggest hits of 1989, doing more than almost all of his previous films to put River Phoenix's name on the lips of casting agents throughout Hollywood. It was a break away from the parts he'd been playing - a more playful role, with plenty of humour and a definite action-adventure emphasis. The film was only second in box office taking to that year's phenomenal success story, Tim Burton's gothic reworking of the dark knight, *Batman* (1989).

One unexpected result of the opening sequence of *Indiana Jones and the Last Crusade* was a spin-off TV series, *The Young Indiana Jones Chronicles*. This lavish and expensive series was created by George Lucas to follow further exploits in the career of the younger version of Indiana Jones introduced in the film. First choice for the TV series role was, of course, River Phoenix. However, he didn't hesitate to turn the part down, fearing that a return to television would have a dire effect on his burgeoning film career, even in a series as big-budgeted and high profile as *The Indiana Jones Chronicles.*

It was at about this time that Arlyn and John Phoenix decided it was time to remove their family, including the nineteen-year-old Phoenix, from the temptations that might await a young star in a shark-infested industry like the movies. 'We consciously got out of Hollywood and moved back to Florida,' said Arlyn. 'We couldn't do it until we knew River was famous enough so that we could go away and he would still be offered parts.'

So late in 1988 the Phoenix family returned to Florida, their landing point upon their return to the United States from their South American adventures. They settled on a 20 acres site in the small town of Micanopy, with a population of just 600, located eight miles south of Gainesville. Gainesville is a classic college town, with the University of Florida located in its midst.

The new Phoenix house, which they had built for them, was described as full of tapestries, Greenpeace posters and Gaia books, reflecting the beliefs of the whole family. The 'compound', known locally as Camp Phoenix, is at the end of a dirt track leading from Route 441 through Florida. The wooden house set in ten acres with a small stream running through it, has three big bedrooms upstairs, one which doubles as an office/parents room, one which Leaf and River were to share upon first moving back out to Florida and the third which Rain, Summer and Liberty, the three Phoenix girls, shared between them. Privacy was obviously not seen as an issue in the Phoenix family. John Phoenix retired from managing his son's career to plant a huge organic garden for their own food, while Arlyn took full control of the film careers of the Phoenix children, including the budding new actors in the family.

It wasn't long, however, before Phoenix decided to move out of the new family ranch, the first real sign that he was asserting his independence from his family. He acquired a two-storey property in Gainesville, only a few miles from Camp Phoenix. 'We are so used to moving it is hard to make a commitment to buying a home,' he said. 'Part of us says we need the stability and also we should invest the money.' Phoenix found life in Florida to be an escape from the pressures of his Hollywood career: 'I've spent so much time in big cities that Gainesville is a relief.'

His sister Rain, who studied Italian at the local university in Gainesville, seemed to be more worried by her brother's fame than he himself was. 'Sometimes I feel more of the frustration than he does. Like, people coming up to him and stuff. It almost makes me more crazed at times. Like God! Why can't they leave him alone, he's just a person.' River himself was less bothered. 'Sometimes I hear stuff like "Hey man, where's your skateboard, dude?" from people who think I'm Christian Slater.'

The move to Gainesville had further complicated Phoenix's relationship with Martha Plimpton. Plimpton was pursuing her film career as actively as Phoenix. Since *The Mosquito Coast* she'd been seen in Andrei Konchalovsky's

*Never far away, River's mother Arlyn supporting her son
at the Oscar ceremony.*

Shy People (1987), *Stars and Bars* (1988) with Daniel Day Lewis, as well as in Woody Allen's *Another Woman* (1988) and *Stanley and Iris* (1990) with Jane Fonda and Robert De Niro. It was also clear that like many young men of his age, River could be fickle. Jane Hallaren, who played River's screen mother in *A Night in the Life of Jimmy Reardon*, recalled a brief encounter featuring Phoenix. 'I have this funny memory of catching him in the hallway with a girl – I won't say whom – and he was going with someone else at the time. He said, "Don't tell anybody, okay?" Like, yeah, I'm going to call his girl-friend. But that was River. Whenever you thought you had him pigeon-holed, he was someone else.'

Martha also acted alongside Phoenix's brother, Leaf, in the Steve Martin comedy *Parenthood* (1989), which also featured Keanu Reeves - the first time Phoenix met the actor with whom he was to work in two films. The whole Phoenix brood were now actors. His sisters Liberty and Summer had appeared in the TV movie *Kate's Secret* (1986), Leaf had been in *Parenthood*, the feeble comedy *Spacecamp* (1986) and *Russkies* (1987), which had co-starred his nine-year-old sister Summer, (who beat his other sister Liberty, eleven, to the role). Rain got in on the act, too, with her debut coming in the comedy *Maid to Order* (1987), opposite Ally Sheedy and Beverly D'Angelo. However, neither Leaf, who had the most success, nor his sisters, was ever to rival the fame and success in films of their eldest brother.

It was in Gainesville that River Phoenix was to develop his musical ambitions, playing guitar and recording, playing gigs in a local venue, the Club Demolition, where the entrance fee goes to the feminist Women's Health Centre, and it was where he was to meet the new woman in his life, Suzanne Solgot, four years his senior.

Chapter 6

As THE 1990s began, River Phoenix found himself facing a crisis in his career. He was now too old to play the teenage heartthrob characters of *A Night in the Life of Jimmy Reardon*, *Little Nikita*, and *Running On Empty*, and the child rites-of-passage roles of *Stand By Me* and *The Mosquito Coast* were long behind him. Yet he wasn't able to secure adult roles either. The heroic adventure of *Indiana Jones and the Last Crusade* was nothing more than an amusing diversion, as Phoenix had a lot of growing to do before he could hope to steal any roles from the likes of Harrison Ford.

Nineteen or twenty is an awkward age to be in the movies. Child star Jodie Foster realised this and took a well judged sabbatical from Hollywood career pressures to attend college - thereby catching up on an interrupted education and getting back in touch with the wider world where her audiences lived and worked. She returned to film-making older, wiser and more able to carve a new direction for herself.

Like Foster, Phoenix also harboured directing ambitions, having always felt more comfortable behind the camera observing rather than in front of it emoting. 'Being an actor you've got to worry about your image all the time. Or at least that's what I'm finding out. A director can sit back and just observe people. I feel more comfortable doing that,' Phoenix had said.

While he was continuing to be offered the teen heart-throb roles, Phoenix wanted to move off in a new direction. He had always harboured an ambition to play in a comedy and was keeping an eye open for a straight 'leading man' role which might provide the much required crossover from teen idol to adult actor. He found the comedy in Lawrence Kasdan's *I Love You To Death* (1990) and an offbeat, leading role in Nancy Savoca's *Dogfight* (1991).

I Love You To Death is a very black farce that received a mixed response upon its release. It tells the tale of a womanising Italian-American Pizza restaurant owner whose wife plots to kill him. Joey Boca, however, is made

The beginning of the 1990s saw River poised on the brink of a serious adult career.

of strong stuff and refuses to die, even after avoiding a bomb in his car, surviving being poisoned with sleeping pills in his spaghetti and even shot in
the head. Finally, a pair of spaced-out hit men are called in to finish the job,
but they turn out to be as incompetent as the family at getting rid of the inde-
structible Joey. Based on true events in the lives of Anthony and Frances
Toto and Barry Giacobe, *I Love You To Death* was just too blackly comic for
some audiences.

The true story that inspired the film first came to the attention of producer Ron Moler in 1984, when he heard the story of the five unsuccessful
attempts on Tony's life by his jealous wife who had discovered his infideli-
ties. The couple had reunited after Frances Toto served out a jail term. He
began to develop the material as a feature film, with his co-producer Patrick
Wells and screenwriter John Kostmayer.

In the middle of this surreal melange of love and attempted murder,
River Phoenix plays Devo Nod, friend and distant admirer of Rosalie
(Tracey Ullman), the wronged wife of philandering Joey Boca (Kevin Kline).
Phoenix couldn't be better cast, as Devo is a nineties New Age New Man,
dressing like an unreformed hippie and uttering dialogue about fate and the
power of crystals.

'*I Love You To Death* is about a pizzeria owner who runs around with
women, until his wife, with the help of his cook, tries to kill him,' said
Phoenix of the film. 'They try five times, but he survives and they get together again. It's a kind of "how to try to kill your husband and save your marriage," but it's based on a true story. I play Devo, a cook who's very mystical,
into Eastern philosophy. I'm the middle man who helps to arrange the
extreme acts that happen in the movie. It's emotional and even moral, even
though it's so dark. They're all victims of ignorance. Devo is overly taken by
details in life, to the point where he can't see the overall picture.'

Despite his peace-and-love philosophy, Devo finds himself drawn into
the plot to murder Joey, due to his affection for Rosalie. After all, he spends
the first few scenes of the movie trying to warn Kline's Joey Boca away from
other women and tries to explain the hurt that would be caused to Rosalie if
she ever found out. Devo, in his wacky wardrobe of outfits, is the opposite of
Joey, the traditional to the point of caricature Italian-American male chau-
vinist pig. They are paired up for much of the film, however, with Phoenix
playing the role of the voice of reason, cautioning Kline's Joey about his illic-
it liaisons.

However, Phoenix drops out of the middle section of the film as Tracey
Ullman and Joan Plowright (as her distraught Yugoslavian mother, Nadja)
take centre stage to plan Joey's death and attempt to carry it out.

Phoenix triumphantly reappears, however, when he is called in by the
amateur murderous pair, to try and finish Joey off. Having never shot

anyone before, he is reluctant and retreats to the kitchen to 'collect himself'. Deciding to do the deed, Devo closes his eyes at the crucial moment and isn't sure if he has hit anything at all, never mind the comatose target lying on the bed.

Devo decides the only way to deal with the situation is to call in a couple of hit men to finish the job off. Donning a fake Fu Manchu moustache, Devo trawls the bars roping in a couple of spaced out would-be killers, Harlon and Marlon James played by cameo players William Hurt and Keanu Reeves.

'They look like drug addicts,' says Plowright's Nadja. 'They are drug addicts,' confirms Phoenix's Devo. 'What did you expect?'

This section of the film contains some of the most hilarious scenes, as Devo tries to co-ordinate the actions of the out-of-this-world pair. Their conversation is full of pregnant pauses and unfinished sentences, with Hurt waving away invisible flies that are bothering him. These cameos are the star turn of the film, and some reviewers noted that Phoenix lost out slightly, having to play it fairly straight opposite two unashamed scene stealers.

The film ends with the local police discovering all is not well with the Joey Boca household and rounding up the entire gang, dragging them off to jail. However, every member of the family admits to trying to kill Joey on their own with no help from anyone else, while Joey's mother (British actress Miriam Margolyes) lays into him in hospital for playing around on his wife. Joey realises that if his wife loves him enough to kill him rather than share him with other women, then his marriage might just be worth saving. The highly improbable conclusion sees Joey bailing everyone, including the hit men, out of jail and dropping all charges, preparing to put more effort into his marriage. Truly a morality tale for the 90s.

Filming on *I Love You To Death* began on location in Tacoma, Washington on 10th April 1989, with Lawrence Kasdan attempting to give the background of the film an industrial, small town feeling which isn't that evident in the finished film. Various buildings in and around Tacoma provided the sets for the pizza restaurant, the Rosalie Villas, owned by Joey, and the police station. After this location work was completed, the entire company returned to Hollywood to film the interior of the Boca house and several smaller sets at the Raleigh Studios.

I Love You To Death is by no means a totally successful film, but it didn't really deserve the critical vilification with which it was greeted. Many reviewers seemed uncomfortable with a film which focused for so much of its time on an attempt to kill someone, and the fact that this was supposed to be a comedy made it even worse. It was a topic that Phoenix and the rest of the cast treated with some humour on the set. 'It might encourage people to go around killing people as a pastime,' he said at the time. 'We discussed it in rehearsal.'

Rolling Stone said the cast of *I Love You To Death* 'hams wickedly...Kline overworks his performance as much as his Italian accent; he's a caricature. Kasdan has inexplicably reduced flesh-and-blood characters to cartoons.' *The Village Voice* suggested the film could be called 'a comedy of remarriage...If I'd found the movie half-way amusing I would make the case. Devo (River Phoenix, still at an awkward age), [is] an earnest hippie who's devoted to Rosalie...'

In *I Love You To Death*, River Phoenix was again sharing the screen with an ensemble cast of widely experienced performers. Kevin Kline was a good role model for him, able with equal ability to turn his hand to drama (in *The January Man*) and comedy (*A Fish Called Wanda*). However, like his character Devo, he was more taken with British comic actress Tracey Ullman than with Kevin Kline. Ullman had first come to prominence on British television and had great success in the United States with her own show on the Fox network. *I Love You To Death* was her most successful film experience, and no doubt she was helped by the other British talents around her - Joan Plowright and Miriam Margolyes, who were particularly picked out for praise in reviews of the film.

'Tracey Ullman and I clicked especially well,' admitted Phoenix of his experience on *I Love You To Death*. 'We had a really good time. We'd just mouth off and get clever on each other and play word games and stuff. And I learned such a lot during filming. I mean, the amount of learning experience from this project would probably equal, you know, the sum of all the other films I've done.'

One of the useful practical skills Phoenix learned on the set was how to make pizza. Although he is only seen in the restaurant cooking briefly at the beginning of the film, director Lawrence Kasdan insisted on extended improvisation sessions for the whole cast, to build a feeling of camaraderie among the characters. This way of working allowed for the free flowing interplay among the family members and the hit men characters evident in the finished film.

I Love You To Death resembles a stage farce, with much of the action confined to one or two locations and mostly taking place through one evening. Extended rehearsals were therefore appropriate, allowing the actors to concentrate on performance, rather than playing to the technical aspects of cinema, as Phoenix had done on *Indiana Jones and the Last Crusade*.

Developing his characters was very important to Phoenix, who would try his best to adapt to the lifestyle and thoughts of the characters he played. With Devo Nod this wasn't too difficult, as the character echoed many aspects of Phoenix's own life and beliefs. 'I don't confuse myself with the characters I play,' he said. 'I make that a really strict point. Anyway, Devo is such a psychological mess-up. He's got a twisted idea of spiritual things and

*In I Love You To Death River Phoenix's role as Devo Nod
was almost an extension of his own 'new age' image*

River cooking pizza in I Love You To Death. In the
interests of screen reality director Lawrence Kasdan made
sure River really learnt how to make them.

all that crystal stuff. He's so serious about life.'

Phoenix could almost be talking about himself in his previous public incarnation of the vegan, earth-loving, nature-protecting, sensitive New Man who just happened to be a rich Hollywood actor. As Phoenix struggled to find a direction in his career, he was also growing ever more tired of his holier-than-thou image and finding it very difficult to keep up the public front that this media manipulation required. 'I feel sorry for the hippies who have to deal with me in the press as their poster child,' he said revealingly. 'I'm certainly not a good example of the pure American hippy.'

At the same time, Phoenix was becoming more and more serious about his work, more concerned with his abilities. He was afflicted with that which plagues many successful actors - doubt. Acting is a very insecure profession. Those actors who are not huge bankable stars able to green light a movie with their name alone (there are very few - Arnold Schwarzenegger, Kevin Costner and Clint Eastwood are among them) find themselves at the mercy of casting directors. Would Phoenix secure another interesting and challenging part after this one? What if the roles began to dry up as he lost his teen appeal? Just where was his career to go as he entered his 20s and was moving away from the control his parents had exercised over his career to date? He had, after all, made two of his worst movies, *A Night in the Life of Jimmy Reardon* and *Little Nikita* more out of fear than anything else.

Actress Miriam Margolyes recognised this quandary in the young actor: 'He's definitely not a kid in this one [*I Love You To Death*]. He's a young man and he's serious and more thoughtful about his work. At the moment he has no way of distancing himself from a part. He is a wonderful actor - as the teenage girls who lined up to get his autograph everywhere we went will tell you.'

Those teenage girl fans were in for a further shock from River Phoenix as he struck out in a new direction with his first leading man role in Nancy Savoca's *Dogfight* (1991). Phoenix was to play a Marine, a thought to make his female fans drool. However, this was to be in a Vietnam film that goes nowhere near a battlefield and further more, he was to fall in love with an ugly duckling aspiring folk singer in 1963 San Francisco.

Dogfight was a dream project for River Phoenix. It was unconventional, yet romantic, quiet yet dramatic. Phoenix pushed himself in *Dogfight* and the result is easily the best performance of his career, including *My Own Private Idaho*, which followed a year later. Screenwriter Bob Comfort based his tale on experiences from his own life. The 'dog fight' of the title is a ritual carried out by Marines on their last night before shipping out to Vietnam. The group throw money into a pot and set out on the town on a mission: to find the ugliest girls in the city and bring them to a wild party. Whoever manages to get

*River Phoenix and Lili Taylor in a tender moment from
Dogfight, when the young Marine realizes that he has
developed a real affection for his 'plain Jane' date.*

the ugliest girl around (an award voted on by a panel of Marine judges) wins the pot.

With such an unpromising sounding plot it's little wonder that Comfort's script languished in Hollywood in trays for over five years, waiting for the right combination of studio, director and stars to make the whole project click into place. Producer Peter Newman carried the film through two studio deals which fell apart before Warner Brothers picked it up and finally gave the troubled project the green light.

Before a director was attached to the film, River Phoenix was cast as Marine Edward Baines Birdlace who willingly participates in the dog fight, but finds himself falling in love with the girl whom he hooks up with. The casting of Phoenix limited the age range of the actress to be cast opposite him and contributed greatly to the tone and style of the film. *Dogfight* is the clearest example where the casting of Phoenix for his star name and status alone significantly affected the direction of the film. Writer Bob Comfort for one had envisaged the central Marine character to be an older figure.

The problem of a suitable director was solved when Newman brought on board Nancy Savoca, director of the low budget feature *True Love* (1989). That film starred Annabella Sciorra and Ron Eldard as a couple caught up in the hassles of an Italian wedding in the Bronx. Very much a slice-of-life film, *True Love* marked out Savoca as a talent to watch.

When brought in to *Dogfight*, Nancy Savoca quickly finalised the second lead role, that of Rose, the plump would-be folk singer. Actress Lili Taylor had in fact auditioned for three different directors for three different previous versions of the film while it languished in development hell, before Savoca was attached to the film and quickly confirmed her in the role.

The $8 million budget that Savoca had at her disposal was far more than the independent film maker had previously handled, but she resisted the temptation to chock the film with Birdlace's Vietnam experiences, despite preparing for it by watching a glut of Vietnam action movies. Savoca decided to follow the more personal and subjective story of Eddie Birdlace, leaving his battlefield experiences mostly off screen.

Phoenix himself was aware of the freshness of having a woman tackle a Vietnam film, hoping that a different perspective on the subject would produce a very different kind of film: 'It's a dichotomy in that we've got a woman director. The norm would be to think, "What's a woman doing directing a film about Marines?".' It is unlikely that Phoenix would have tackled a more straightforward Vietnam film - he would never have taken on the Charlie Sheen role in Oliver Stone's *Platoon* (1986), for example.

Although set in San Francisco, Bronx-bred Savoca shot *Dogfight* in Seattle and managed to keep Warner Brothers studio executives at arm's length. Studios are always quick to co-opt developing talent from the independent

sector to the studio system, but most fail to realise that if they want the talent to perform successfully, a hands-off approach is the most successful way to go. Pleased with the casting of the increasingly popular and critically acclaimed River Phoenix in the central role, the studio was however worried that his buzz-cut Marine hairstyle might put off his female following or even render the young actor near to unrecognisable. The studio, therefore, insisted on blond highlights in River's cropped hair (as it turns out these are nearly invisible on screen). Lili Taylor also had to undergo some cosmetic changes to play the part of Rose including padding to enlarge the not-plump-enough actress and a high-calorie diet to help her pile on the pounds.

Despite the fact that once more Phoenix was playing a part that seemed ideally suited to him, the actor was again at great pains to distance himself from the character on screen. 'There are things in the film that Birdlace does that if it were me, I'd be so embarrassed. But it's not me, it completely belongs to him.'

Having said that, though, Phoenix did go to great lengths to get into the character. Director Savoca arranged an abbreviated boot camp experience for Phoenix and the other actors who play Marines in the film. Two former drill instructors put the actors through their paces for five days, on Vashon Island, ironically enough a hippie commune close to Seattle.

Savoca was keen for her actors to not only look like Marines, talk like Marines and act like Marines, but to experience something of what it must be like to train as a Marine. 'It's a way for me to get these guys who would probably never want to be in the military at all to understand the pride that Marines take in their survival of Boot Camp. They came out of there an incredible unit. I mean, it was scary, the way they bonded. And it was exactly what was needed. I wanted to get those details right.'

Co-star Anthony Clark described how the experience of boot camp affected River: 'On the first night we're out of boot camp we went to this party, and it ended up that the police were called. River was the head of that whole thing. He had a mean streak. He wanted to get into a fight. That night he was a Marine.'

Dogfight is structured as an extended flashback, opening with the older Birdlace limping back home to San Francisco. On the cross-country bus trip, he recalls the experiences of his final night in the United States before shipping out to the war in Vietnam. It is November 1963, mere days before the assassination of President John F. Kennedy while his motorcade crossed Dealy Plaza in downtown Dallas. Four Marines, among them Birdlace and group leader Berzin, split up in San Francisco to hunt down suitable women to take along to the dog fight in the hope of winning the cash in the pot. Phoenix has his 'charming' persona to the fore as he attempts to pick up one woman after another, only to become short-tempered and foul-mouthed as

River, who was an accomplished guitarist, re-kindled his interest in music when he moved from Los Angeles to Gainesville in Florida.

105

one attempt fails after another. It is the eve of his nineteenth birthday.

He meets Rose in the cafe run by her mother, where she is strumming on her guitar in the corner. Birdlace goes into bulishit overdrive in an attempt to get a conversation going about folk music, in which Rose has a clear interest. After first refusing to accompany him to the 'party', the nature of which she doesn't know, Rose changes her mind and quickly gets ready, in one of the best sequences of the film.

Rose talks non-stop all the way across town to the party, and by the time they arrive at the night club door, Birdlace is clearly having second thoughts about putting Rose through the ordeal of the dog fight. Phoenix's trademark 'sensitive' persona comes to the fore, as he plays the part of the confused Marine, both playing up to his macho soon-to-be comrades in arms and trying to wrestle with the thoughts and feelings he is unexpectedly discovering for Rose. These moments are subtle, wrapped as they are in the advancing narrative of the film, but they show Phoenix quietly at work, developing themes and thoughts that will recur later in the film. Failing to talk Rose out of going into the night club and failing to prevent her from dancing, Birdlace is a willing recipient of her justified anger when she discovers the true nature of the party: 'You're a cruel, heartless, ignorant creep.'

Failing to lose his thoughts of Rose in a pinball arcade, Birdlace quickly leaves his Marine buddies to return to Rose's home and tries to get to see her again, comically overcoming the intervention of a hungry guard dog in the process. Confused about his own feelings and why he has returned to apologise, an act not in his nature, Birdlace persuades Rose to give him one more chance and accompany him on '...a regular date. Two regular people on a regular date.' It is then that the true romance of *Dogfight* begins.

Three years later and Birdlace is the only one of the foursome to return from Vietnam, to a very changed United States. In his military fatigues, Birdlace now finds himself a figure of hate as he walks the streets rather than a hero: 'How many babies did you kill?' demands a passing hippy. Confronted with a flood of unusual sights and sounds, Birdlace takes refuge in a bar across from Rose's coffee shop, before working up the courage to return and see her. The film ends with their extended, silent embrace.

River Phoenix was never conventional in his selection of projects, and *Dogfight* is no exception. The young actor takes great risks with his perceived heart-throb persona, while at the same time trading on that persona. Who among his fans wouldn't want to see River Phoenix as a sensitive Marine, but then to twist that and have him falling in love with a woman who doesn't have the looks of a Californian model is to confound audience expectations. That choice brought Phoenix a little closer to the ordinary lives of his fans, too. If Rose could manage to sweep Phoenix off his feet, then anyone in the audience stood a chance. It made a celluloid hero just that little bit more human.

Dogfight is laced with period pop and folk music, making for a tapestry that reflects the dramatic changes between 1963 and 1966, from the death of Kennedy to the blossoming of the flower power era. A quiet, understated film, nevertheless *Dogfight* deals with the issue of Vietnam in as strong and forceful a way as the more obvious *Platoon* or *Casualties of War* (1989). *Dogfight* concentrates on the personal and the home front rather than the impersonal nature of battle in a foreign land.

The Village Voice had its reservations about it, but did comment 'Director Nancy Savoca gets typically strong performances from Phoenix and Taylor.' *Variety*, meanwhile, thought that *Dogfight* 'underplays the character development to such an extent that the film has a muted, very modest impact.' It called the screenplay 'surprisingly benign...intermittently intriguing...'

By-passing cinemas in Britain, *Dogfight* went straight out on video release, becoming a cult success in the process. Jo Berry in *Empire* wrote of *Dogfight* as 'River Phoenix's best kept secret...[He is] possibly Hollywood's finest young leading man. Phoenix yet again displays all the signs of a potential master at work.'

Dogfight wasn't the only thing River Phoenix was secretive about; in reality he had other preoccupations which he needed to keep hidden. A friend of Martha Plimpton's alleged that she finally broke off the relationship with Phoenix soon after the 1989 Oscar ceremony because he had begun to dabble in the world of drugs. Whether this was true or not, the year before Phoenix had anyway started a relationship in Florida with Suzanne Solgot, a 26-year-old massage therapist and musician.

Phoenix began to pursue his growing musical ambitions with ever more vigour at the end of the 1980s. Freed from the constant supervision of his parents, living in his own rented house in Gainesville, he started a belated teen rebellion, becoming more and more attracted to the lifestyle of the rock musicians he met at the Club Demolition in Gainesville and those hanging out on the LA club scene.

Phoenix started his own band, named Aleka's Attic, which featured his sister Rain, and played in The Hardback Cafe in Gainesville, among other places. It was in these circles that he met Suzanne Solgot (whom he called Sue) who played in an all-girl punk band. These interests and events were to gradually lay the seeds of River Phoenix's downfall.

The combined worlds of music and movies, with the free availability of drugs and the ever-increasing career pressures under which Phoenix found himself, seem to have conspired to set him off on a two and a half year descent into growing drug abuse, which was finally to lead to his untimely death in 1993.

Chapter 7

FOR HIS next two films River Phoenix was to set out the approach he intended to take to his mature film career, attempting to combine the challenging art house role of a gay hustler in *My Own Private Idaho* (1991) with the lighter demands of appearing as part of an ensemble in the mainstream hit in *Sneakers* (1992).

My Own Private Idaho was a pet project of independent American director Gus Van Sant. Emerging from a well off middle class family, Van Sant found himself living as a struggling film-maker in Hollywood, fascinated by the street life of the town. 'It was a secret world I knew nothing about,' he says of the inspiration for the slim storyline. Previously Van Sant had made the prize winning *Mala Noche* (1985), about a grocery clerk's infatuation with a Mexican migrant worker, and the acclaimed *Drugstore Cowboy* (1989), which starred Matt Dillon as the leader of a gang of junkies who raid drugstores for supplies. The film scooped the 1989 National Society of Film Critics awards for Best Film, Best Director, and Best Screenplay.

With a script ready for *My Own Private Idaho*, mixing the lowlife world of the street with a plot and mannerisms borrowed from Shakespeare's Henry IV parts one and two, Van Sant had to face the tough job of casting the central parts of the two street hustlers from Portland, Oregon. Van Sant sent the completed script out to River Phoenix, asking him to consider the leading role of Mike Waters, a male prostitute who suffers from narcolepsy, a condition which means he falls into a deep, coma-like sleep whenever he's put under undue stress. Mike drifts through the film in a half-hearted search for the mother who abandoned him, struggling to survive on the streets. Van Sant also sent a copy of the script out to Keanu Reeves, offering him the role of Scott Favor, a modern Prince Hal, who is slumming it on the streets while waiting to come into his inheritance, and the object of Mike's unreciprocated love.

These actors were radical choices for such offbeat and non-mainstream

River Phoenix as Mike during the funeral scene in My Own Private Idaho. He was prepared to take a risk with his image in playing a the part of a gay hustler in this film.

roles in a film which was bound to be controversial and was already worrying executives at New Line Cinema (the production company behind the amazingly successful Freddy Krueger *Nightmare on Elm Street* films). New Line were in the process of branching out into more 'art house' film production and had agreed to make the film, but certain explicit scenes in *My Own Private Idaho* caused them concern.

Van Sant himself admits that he sent the scripts out to Phoenix and Reeves never really believing that these 'teen idol' actors would actually say 'yes' to the controversial roles. 'I assumed that their agents would say "No", but as we began to talk to River and Keanu, it became clearer that they were up to the challenge.'

Gus Van Sant said that *My Own Private Idaho* was 'the story of a rich boy who falls off the hill and a kid on the street. I saw a bit of the hill in Keanu's personality and a bit of the street in River's. They played out these extensions of themselves.'

Phoenix and Reeves themselves did have doubts about taking on the roles, but ended up egging each other on to take the plunge and commit to the project. 'We just forced ourselves into it. We said "OK, I'll do it if you do it. I won't do it if you won't." We shook hands, that was it.'

However, considering that Van Sant managed to draw out the best performance Matt Dillon has yet given on film in *Drugstore Cowboy*, how could the young actors resist the opportunity Van Sant was presenting them, with similarly unconventional material. For River Phoenix, *My Own Private Idaho* was exactly the kind of out-of-left-field project that would interest the young actor. Fiercely determined to keep his performances fresh by constantly challenging himself, Phoenix was not primarily concerned with how his many teenage female fans might react upon seeing him playing a male prostitute. Similarly, he didn't seem that worried about the effect taking on the role might have on his film career either.

'I decide my projects not based on any big strategy or how Hollywood or the critics will see me,' said Phoenix at the time. 'If you have a belief in the story, you'll just commit. You don't think "What will people think of this?" If you do, you're ruined.'

Before filming began, Phoenix was asked about his reasons for taking on such an unexpected role and how he would tackle the controversial sex scenes. 'It's quite cruel and hardcore,' he said. 'But I decided it was a beautiful story. One of the opening scenes with a male prostitute going about his job is pretty graphic. And I asked the director why it was there, if it wasn't just sensational? But what these characters do has to be shown. It won't be glamorised at all.'

So Phoenix followed his instincts and took on the role of Mike, eventually turning in what would be regarded by most critics as one of his best per-

River playing with Aleka's Attic at the Rock Against Fur benefit in 1989.

River Phoenix as rent boy Mike about to collapse into a
narcoleptic coma in the company of Alena (Grace
Zabriskie), in My Own Private Idaho.

formances. Nevertheless, it was inevitable that playing in such a film would find Phoenix at the centre of a wider controversy. Hollywood, represented by its creative personnel, the actors, writers and directors, seems uncomfortable with films featuring gay characters or homosexual sex. It took many years for films to deal with the subject at all, and even longer for the spectre of AIDS (ironically, a disease so visible among the Hollywood creative community) to be dealt with by mainstream film.

For these reasons, playing a hustler in a 'gay' film was not what was expected of one of Hollywood's young rising stars. 'For sensational reasons people might say this is about gay street life, which is really great for the gay community because it's important to have something to identify with. But it doesn't necessarily represent the gay community. You don't hear about *Five Easy Pieces* [1970] as a film about a guy who works on an oil rig and he's heterosexual.'

As always, Phoenix had his liberal credentials to the fore in his views on the relevance of *My Own Private Idaho* to the subjects and lifestyles depicted in the cinema of the nineties: 'It might take a few of these films before there's, like, a natural stride with the whole issue and then maybe one day it won't even be an issue, which is what I'm hoping.'

Gus Van Sant was more emphatic, believing the film was more about prostitution rather than some underground gay street life, and that the character played by River Phoenix was central to the film: 'It's a film about an area of society - prostitution - that's not defined in terms of gay or straight. River's character may be gay, but you're not really sure - he's not really sure. And the hustlers and the johns don't think of themselves as gay. In real life the clients for these street hustlers tend to be middle-class businessmen or construction workers with families.'

Phoenix and Reeves play Mike and Scott, part of a street gang of prostitutes who hang out in a derelict hotel. Leader of the bunch is the older Bob Pigeon, a kind of Falstaff to Reeves' Prince Hal. The part of Pigeon is played by William Richert, director of *A Night in the Life of Jimmy Reardon*.

Throughout the film Scott is Mike's protector, taking care of him when narcolepsy renders Mike unconscious, endangering both his life and his income. Scott is only on the streets temporarily, though, intending to clean up his act upon turning 21 and inheriting his family fortune. Then he will turn his back on the low-life world of sex-for-money and move in the exalted realms of politics and high finance. Mike has no such escape from the harsh realities of life on the street. Scott helps him out in his search for his lost mother, until in Rome he suddenly falls in love with an Italian girl and turns his back on Mike.

The film ends with two funerals, that of Scott's real father, the Mayor of Portland, and of his one-time father-of-the-streets, Bob Pigeon. The worlds of the two dead men and their respective funerals couldn't be further apart. While Scott solemnly carries out his family duties with his new Italian wife, Mike is to be found with the street gang dancing on Bob's grave, before he once more hits the road (literally, as narcolepsy takes a grip once more at the film's finale).

My Own Private Idaho is an unconventional movie, with two young stars playing unconventional roles. The film, though, clearly belongs to River Phoenix. The initial focus is on the character of Mike, introducing the viewer to the world of the film and it is with Phoenix's little boy lost that the viewer's sympathies stay. On the other hand, in common with many of his other movies, Keanu Reeves seems more to react rather than act. Throughout the film, Phoenix is the more believable of the two, living a role that may have had more similarities with his then real life than most critics and reviewers suspected. The two young men did become good friends, however. 'River is my buddy, dude,' said Reeves in a joint interview to publicise the film. 'I've always loved you, River. River is my best friend and, to be honest, I don't have many of them.'

The key scene between them comes about halfway through, when Mike and Scott are stuck on the road with a broken down, stolen motorcycle. They are sitting by a campfire when Phoenix's Mike haltingly begins to declare his love for Reeve's Scott. Curled up in front of the fire, rocking gently to-and-fro, and hugging himself, Phoenix makes the most of the moment, with Reeves merely a blank, reactive slate, there to be the recipient of Phoenix's character-defining dialogue. The scene is the most touching in the film and provides countless clues to the interior depths of the character of Mike.

Gus Van Sant was impressed with Phoenix's handling of the role, and with the fact that the young actor took it upon himself to rewrite the dialogue, giving a different emphasis to the scene. 'River makes it more like he's attracted to his friend,' said Van Sant, 'that he's really in love with him. Yes, that he's in love with him. He made the whole character that way, whereas I wrote the character as more out of it, more myopic.'

For Keanu Reeves however the scene was a bit of an ordeal. 'I'm not against gays or anything, but I won't have sex with guys. I would never do that on film. We did a little of it in "Idaho" and, believe me, it was hard work. Never again.'

Phoenix saw connections between this scene in *My Own Private Idaho* and scenes in his other movies, giving him a concrete reference point for the dynamics of the scene. 'You don't know until you see the dailies whether it's come across or not. Because we shot in sequence, we were watching the film unfold before us and when that scene came around we could just ad-lib to it. [It is similar to] the confession scene in *Stand By Me*. It's also similar to the scene in *Running On Empty*. Gus did see both movies, so maybe he sampled them?'

Phoenix believed that it was Van Sant's relaxed approach to directing the actors that allowed him to furnish such a good performance in *My Own Private Idaho*: 'Gus is very open to collaboration. He doesn't direct in a show-and-tell style but instead asks questions and brings it out of you like a good psychiatrist might. He allows you to be responsible for your role. Directors can be very frightened of collaborative things with actors. When we talked, we cut a deal where I had complete creative control. I was curious because I had a lot of input and he was very open about my suggestions. So this collaboration became my apprenticeship with Gus.'

Phoenix found he was acting the part of the often unconscious Mike almost unconsciously himself: 'When I first start working on a role, I really go overboard. I do too much. For about a week, I guess you could say I over-act. Then for about three days I just think about my lines...each word. Everything is very literal. Once I start filming, I let everything go. I try to forget everything I've done and be as simple as possible. In simplicity there is truth.'

He put many hours of research into his part in the $2.5 million film. 'I spent quite a few hours on the streets in Portland between eight and four in the morning.' He would find where the trade among the traffic was going on and hang out with the other kids on the street, who didn't seem to realise they had a rising Hollywood star in their midst. 'If anything, they thought "this is another cat who's trying to take my spot on the street". There was maybe a little curiosity, but never any animosity or jealousy.'

Phoenix would target cars and try to catch the attention of the drivers, as Mike would have to do in the film. 'The next step would be just to open the door and get in. That's when I'd tell them to fuck off.' It is possible that Phoenix's immersion in the role went too far. Certain Gus Van Sant had his fears for Phoenix. 'He sort of assumes the character. He seemed to be changing into this character.' This was an observation reinforced by Eric Allan Edwards, the director of photography on *My Own Private Idaho*. 'He looked like a street kid. In a very raw way he wore that role. I've never seen anybody so intent on living his role.'

Despite his research and hard work on the role, Phoenix wasn't sure what he'd done with the part until he saw the finished film. 'The hardest part is fully believing what you have concocted after all the research is done. Sometimes it just doesn't happen and then, suddenly, you're there. I didn't realise what I had done until way after the film was over.'

If Phoenix didn't realise the strength of his performance, others did. The actor found himself the toast of the Venice Film Festival that year, with his performance in *My Own Private Idaho* securing him the Best Actor award. River was happy to credit the virtues of the performance to his director. 'Gus

Van Sant is a beautiful person,' said Phoenix. 'Every day of my life since I finished *My Own Private Idaho*, at some point in the day, I find the conversation somehow goes back to that film, because it was such a great experience. I just start getting all joyous about it and babbling about it...'

The critics were enamoured of the film, too, with Philip Thomas in *Empire* magazine realising Phoenix's centrality to the whole project, describing his performance as 'excellent': 'Despite the often ludicrous situations in which he is required to emote, Phoenix really is frighteningly convincing as the screwed up hustler looking for direction and the love of the self-seeking Reeves.' *Variety* agreed with that assessment, commenting: 'Phoenix cuts a believable, sometimes compelling figure of a young man urgently groping for definition in his life.'

Phoenix was to appear in one other Gus Van Sant film, his version of Tom Robbins' novel *Even Cowgirls Get The Blues* (1992). Phoenix featured in a small cameo role as a guru-seeking hippy, with people like William Burroughs and Roseanne Arnold, as a favour to Van Sant. The film featured Rainbow Phoenix in a major role, starring alongside Uma Thurman.

Gus Van Sant and River Phoenix had planned out at least one more project that they hoped to work together on in the near future, a film biography of pop artist Andy Warhol. During a question and answer session for *Interview* Magazine, conducted by River Phoenix, Van Sant started talking about his Warhol project: 'It dawned on me that you look a lot like Warhol did when he was, say, eighteen to 25. It would be a stretch, but you could pull off playing the young Warhol.'

The project wasn't to happen due to Phoenix's death. Neither did the young actor ever get his chance to turn his hand to directing, an interest that was rekindled by his experiences in the making of *My Own Private Idaho*. 'I want to buy a 16mm film camera,' he said at the time. 'I'm not committed to the idea of being a filmmaker, but I'd like to try some shorts. I really like documentaries.'

In 1992 Phoenix returned to more mainstream cinematic pursuits in the ensemble caper movie *Sneakers*. Like the earlier *I Love You To Death*, Phoenix found himself surrounded by a group of old movie hands, led by Robert Redford and Sidney Poitier, whom Phoenix had worked opposite in *Little Nikita* back in 1987. Like his performance in *I Love You To Death*, Phoenix managed to more than hold his own when surrounded by vastly more experienced actors, even managing to up stage some of the older performers.

Phoenix first encountered Robert Redford in connection with the casting of Redford's film *A River Runs Through It* (1992). Based on the autobiographical novel by Norman Maclean about fly-fishing brothers (played by Brad Pitt and Craig Sheffer) and their Presbyterian minister father (Tom Skerrit) in turn of the century Montana, the film was a pet project of Redford's, which he'd opted to direct.

'It's a great script,' said Phoenix of the film, during the casting process. 'Just the best script that I've read that's come out of Hollywood in a long time. I auditioned - me and about a thousand other guys. It was a nice audition and I haven't auditioned in a while. I thought I'd be nervous...I had a really good talk, good meeting with Redford, but I think he's gonna find the guy. The guy who just is that image - the Montana mountain boy, fly fisherman image. That's what I think he should do. I believe so strongly in it, that I want the best guy for it. If I get it, great. If I don't, I wasn't right for it.'

Phoenix didn't get the part. However, the audition process had put Phoenix in touch with Redford, which was to be useful when it came to the *Sneakers* project. *Sneakers* was developed by the screenwriting team of Lawrence Lasker and Walter F. Parkes. The pair had written the hit movie *WarGames* (1983), directed by action specialist John Badham. Matthew Broderick was the teen hero of the movie who managed to hack into the computer defence systems of the United States, almost resulting in 'Global Thermonuclear War'. With a domestic US gross of $74 million, *WarGames* ensured that they would have no trouble getting further scripts produced.

Lasker and Parkes weren't short of ideas for a follow-up, developing the high concept notion of a 'high tech Dirty Dozen' during the research for *WarGames*. It was to be another decade before the film was made, by which time River Phoenix found himself central to the green light being given to the movie by Universal studios.

The scriptwriters worked on the *Sneakers* project with writer-director Phil Alden Robinson, who'd made it to the big time in 1990, writing and directing *Field of Dreams*, a wish fulfilment baseball fantasy starring Kevin Costner. Robinson had been scripting successful films in Hollywood for years, including the Steve Martin vehicle *All of Me* (1984), co-starring Lily Tomlin. Robinson was involved in the *Sneakers* project at an early stage: 'It didn't occur to us that it was taking a long time until we were about six years into the project,' he claims.

'We all loved caper films,' said Robinson. 'We never got bored with the characters [in *Sneakers*], but our storylines ranged from 'Three Days of the Hacker' to 'Raiders of the Lost Computer'.'

This tale of a team of computer wizards who break into company security systems to test how vulnerable they might be needed a charismatic team leader. The character of Martin Bishop was a sixties teen who'd grown up to become a nineties computer rebel. Robert Redford was the automatic choice for the role. 'In my lifetime of movie going,' says Robinson, 'Redford is the best at playing the cool, smart American hero who gets in over his head. Nobody does that combination better than he does. That's Martin Bishop in

Sneakers.'

Robert Redford felt that *Sneakers* promised much, but it was more than just the substantial leading role that got him involved in the film: 'I was intrigued by the topics in *Sneakers*, but part of what interested me in the project was the cast that was shaping up. It was sort of counter-casting and that was fun and exciting.'

Among the major leading characters to be cast was the role of a nineteen year old computer hacker named Carl Arbogast, who had broken into his school computer to increase his grades.

Co-screenwriter Walter F. Parkes recalls the casting of the part of Carl: 'It was pretty clear that the studio would make the movie by the time Redford wanted to make it, even by the time Phil wanted to make it, but it was presented to us as a necessary part of the equation to cast that young actor.'

'That young actor' was the rising star River Phoenix. According to director Phil Alden Robinson, Phoenix was the unanimous first choice for the role. Robinson says of Phoenix: 'He was in the scenes on the first day we shot, and I thought it was OK, but once I saw him on film in the dailies, he was wonderful. He makes very quirky choices that really come alive on film.'

Also in the cast was Sidney Poitier, immediately following Phoenix in the opening credits billing (a reversal of their *Little Nikita* credits); Mary Mac-Donnell, who'd co-starred with Kevin Costner in his directorial debut *Dances With Wolves* (1990) and comedy actor Dan Aykroyd, one of the *Ghostbusters* (1984). Also on board was David Strathairn, a frequent collaborator with director John Sayles. Rounding out this high powered cast was Ben Kingsley, as the villain of the piece, Cosmo.

Phoenix had made a habit throughout his career of working with experienced actors, but even in *Sneakers* he still admitted to being overawed by the more experienced performers. 'Dan and I would stand next to Redford and Poitier on the set sometimes and we'd think, "These guys are like national monuments, like the pyramids." And that poses the question: "But what are we?" Well, I guess we're sand crabs, or something less dignified!'

Production began on *Sneakers* on 28th October 1991 in Oakland, California, just a week after the devastating fire that ravaged the town. The film wrapped in March 1992, two weeks over schedule and slightly over budget. By summer 1992, though, Universal executives had stopped complaining about the overruns, as research screening scores were high enough for the studio to schedule the film quickly for September 1992 release.

Phoenix felt that filming *Sneakers* was somewhat different to his other film experiences. 'It's a wonderful experience, but it doesn't feel like a movie for some reason,' he told *Premiere* magazine. 'The work we do is very technical, and you have to keep the concentration for three, four months. After

River had no difficulty in portraying a gay man in My Own Private Idaho. His co-star Keanu Reeves was more ambivalent.

119

Idaho, I just did not feel like barrelling through someone's psychosis, you know? I needed to do something that didn't involve so much guts.'

Although Phoenix regarded his performance in *Sneakers* as a more relaxing movie role, he was aware of the possible wider perception. 'I play this cyberpunk nerd, just full on. I trashed myself in this. I will never appear in a teen magazine again. I've really degraded myself. He's very hyper, always twitching, the kind of guy you avoid playing if you want to walk with grace and dignity at the premiere. I'm going to, like...I'm not going to go.'

Sneakers opens with two young hackers (the young versions of the Redford and Kingsley characters) breaking into the Federal Reserve computer and transferring funds from the Republican Party to the Black Panthers. Redford's Bishop is out buying the pizzas when the FBI raid the campus and pull in Kingsley's Cosmo. Jumping forward from the analogue sixties to the cyberpunk nineties, we find Bishop has formed a team of computer experts who test security systems, the 'sneakers' of the title. A visit from a pair of National Security Agency men asking Bishop and his team to retrieve a smart black box code breaker from a mysterious professor launches the caper of the film that eventually reunites Bishop and Cosmo. A series of cross and double-cross situations develops, until the 'sneakers' don't know who to trust with the most powerful code breaker yet developed.

Phoenix found himself in the position of stealing scenes - quite literally - from his more experienced co-stars. At the request of director Robinson, Dan Aykroyd was happy to hand over the prime role in a key break-in sequence

River Phoenix (Mike) and Keanu Reeves (Scott) take to the road in search of Mike's mother in My Own Private Idaho.

near the climax of the movie to Phoenix. The sequence ends with Phoenix falling through a suspended ceiling on top of Timothy Busfield, who plays one of Cosmo's heavies. Busfield was no doubt eternally grateful that he had to deal with the younger and lighter Phoenix crashing in on him, rather than the somewhat larger and more rotund Aykroyd.

Phoenix plays the part of Carl Arbogast with a light touch, aiming more for comedy than the heroics that might be expected of the actor who once played the young Indiana Jones. He's especially good in the scenes where he's paired with Redford, playing light relief comedy against the older 'straight man'. The clash between the pair of age and values makes for a good chemistry, which is at the heart of the film.

At one stage when asking Bishop about his past, Phoenix's Carl comments: 'You were taking big chances - what for?'. Not satisfied by Bishop's answers that he was young and there was a war on, Carl finally understands when Bishop comments: 'It was a good way to meet girls.' Both Phoenix and Redford find themselves in this scene playing up to their respective audiences, which although generations apart are looking to both actors for the same things: handsome good looks, a devilish sense of humour and the ability to entertain for a couple of hours.

At the end of the film, Phoenix gets to play up to the teenage girl audience that he felt would not appreciate the almost 'nerdy' role he'd taken on in *Sneakers*. When cutting a deal with James Earl Jones National Security Agency man, the Sneakers team get to ask for what they want most in the world. The requests range from Bishop wanting his record cleared, Poitier wanting a European holiday for his family and David Strathairn's request for 'peace on earth and goodwill to all men' (only to be told that the United States Government doesn't do that kind of thing).

Phoenix's Carl, meanwhile, has been eyeing up the young, female agent in the room who has been training a machine gun on them. 'I'd like the phone number of the young lady with the Uzi,' he says. Amazed, the woman gladly mouths the numbers. How many of Phoenix's legion of young, female fans would wish to be in that position? Clearly, despite Phoenix's slight misgivings about the role, his producers were well aware of the audience that was likely to follow him from film to film.

Phoenix makes the most of his role in *Sneakers*, and although he might seem to be cruising through the movie, his performance was greeted with unanimously good notices. Critic Tom Charity in Britain's *Sight and Sound* magazine clearly felt that the young Phoenix more than held his own up against past masters like Redford and Poitier: 'Bishop is the least interesting of the *Sneakers* dirty half-dozen. Robert Redford has always been a re-active actor, he can't take charge of a scene the way Sidney Poitier does, or register quirky character details like River Phoenix.'

While he had been making *My Own Private Idaho* and *Sneakers*, River Phoenix was realising an ambition with his band, Aleka's Attic. Ever since he and Rain were kids singing for cash on the streets of Caracas, Phoenix had harboured musical ambitions. In his early TV appearances his musical talents took precedence over his developing acting abilities.

His fame in the world of film also proved to be an open door to the exclusive LA clubs, where young film stars would mix with members of the 'indie' rock scene and drug taking was a very big part of the action. Phoenix was lead guitarist and vocalist for Aleka's Attic with his sister Rain and a mutating line up of other rock star wannabes. Playing the rock star was one of Phoenix's escapes from the pressures of the film world and the good-guy image he, his family and his publicists had created for him. Now he was beginning publicly to reject it. He saw the dangers to the environment as cataclysmic but he began to hint that it had little relevance to his personal lifestyle: 'I don't care if people call me a goody-goody nature boy. They can just shove it up their ass. The world's falling in on them. They're just gonna be blind ducklings,' he had said, in a rare outburst.

When not making films, Phoenix would retreat to his home in Gainesville, Florida, near his parents' ranch, where he lived with Sue Solgot. 'When we first met,' she said, 'he seemed really sweet and gentle. At least he's getting some hair now. When I met him he didn't have any hair.'

Despite beginning to reject his image as Hollywood's Mr Clean, Phoenix seems to have regarded his frequent returns to Gainesville as an escape from the hype and hassle of Tinseltown. 'I have a good battery charger at home,' he said. 'I get back into the family and plug in. I'll always want to spend a lot of time at Camp Phoenix.'

Asked how he passed that time, Phoenix was only too happy to supply his, by now standard, 'nature-boy' answer. 'I have some beautiful friends and I like to play guitar and I like to walk in nature. Life is multi-layered and there's no way I could do my life justice in one pat answer.' However, Sue Solgot reported that all was not always sweetness and light in the Phoenix household. 'When he gets mad, he can get pretty crazy,' she said.

Back home in Gainesville, Phoenix would also record music by Aleka's Attic. While the rock'n'roll lifestyle was an escape from his clean and healthy image, Phoenix was fairly serious about his musical ambitions. Not only did he play the music and sing the vocals, but Phoenix was also the band's songwriter. Aleka's Attic was featured on a compilation album, entitled *Tame Yourself*, along with other alternative/independent artists such as Indigo Girls, k. d. lang and the B-52s (The title of the film *My Own Private Idaho* had come from a song by the B-52s.) The album was put together as a benefit piece for People for Ethical Treatment of Animals (PETA).

Phoenix would play at events like Rock Against Fur in 1989 and at vari-

River more than held his own with the high profile cast of Sneakers. Left to right: River Phoenix, Robert Redford, Dan Aykroyd, Sidney Poitier.

ous protest rallies sponsored by PETA. At these events Phoenix lived the best of both worlds, supporting those causes he passionately believed in while playing the bad boy rock star, jamming on his guitar.

Phoenix was keen on keeping a low profile with Aleka's Attic, at leas early on, sometimes changing the band's name to ensure that people came to see the band, rather than coming to see him. 'Aleka is the spirit of the group,' explained Phoenix. Aleka's Attic is a converted guest house on the Phoenix family's Florida ranch, kitted out by Phoenix's musician father John as a practice room cum recording studio. 'This room is Aleka's Attic. Aleka was an imaginary creature who wrote poetry and music and gave up its spirit for the band.'

After filming was completed on *My Own Private Idaho*, Phoenix had taken Aleka's Attic on a three month tour of clubs and colleges on the East Coast of the States, trying to build and maintain an 'underground' reputation for his dabblings in the world of progressive rock. Between *My Own Private Idaho* and his work on *Sneakers*, Phoenix was seriously laying down recordings with Aleka's Attic in the hope of securing a talked-about recording contract with Island Records.

John Lennon was a musical and lifestyle hero for River Phoenix, because of his supposed radical views. Phoenix believed he was a guru-figure for millions of people like himself. 'The fucking asshole who shot Lennon is in some Mafia prison, can you believe it?' he said. 'John Lennon was bumped off because of his pro-environment stand. If John Lennon said, "Turn off your televisions now guys, we'll save electricity for two days straight," three million people instantly in America would've done it. If Lennon would've said, "Please," over the airwaves, "please don't vote for Ronald Reagan" - you're telling me that three million people going in to vote for their President wouldn't have been cancelled out?'

Phoenix's hero worship wasn't without humour, though. With sound engineers complaining 'We'll never whip these guys into shape,' and commenting that the Beatles produced their first album over several days, Phoenix responded: 'Yeah, and what was that? Like, "She loves you, yeah, yeah, yeah." '

One of Phoenix's closest friends from the music world was Michael Balzary, better known as Flea, bassist with the Red Hot Chilli Peppers. The Red Hot Chilli Peppers often played The Viper Room, on LA's Sunset Strip, with co-owner and film star Johnny Depp jamming along with them. Phoenix had got Flea a small part in *My Own Private Idaho*, playing the character of Budd, and the two would often hang out with larger groups in the clubs along Sunset Strip.

One Viper Room regular said of Phoenix: 'He couldn't have cared less about being a movie star. What he really got into was hanging with the musicians, learning from them, playing with them. Almost all of the people he came in here with were musicians.'

Whenever Phoenix was in LA working on a film, he would often take time out, round up a gang and hit the clubs, either to soak up the musical atmosphere, or to take to the stage himself and play. Phoenix had disbanded the original Gainesville line-up of Aleka's Attic and reformed the band in LA, though Rain remained part of it. This was exactly the kind of lifestyle that the Phoenix family had hoped to avoid by moving back out to Florida almost as soon as their eldest son had become established as a film actor. Arlyn said, 'We saw what was happening to other children and we said "That's no way to raise kids". Drew Barrymore [child star of *E.T.*] got caught up in it. You could see her at nine years old at awards parties. All that becomes more important than life. And it is Hollywood that does it to people. It happened to Charlie Sheen and to lots of others. It's the drugs. It changes you so quickly that you can't get hold of yourself.'

The anti-drugs line had been part of the Children of God sermons that Phoenix recalled from his early years in Venezuela. 'We heard Janis Joplin shot airplane glue into her veins the night she died, that's the kind of stuff the pastor would tell us. "Cocaine - the devil's dandruff". I think I might wait until I'm 70 and then do it all at once,' he said disingenuously. 'Just stay ultra-healthy till I'm seventy and then just go, "Waaaaaa-oooooo!"'

Despite the protective attitudes of his family and his own professed dislike of the entire drug scene, it was at this time that Phoenix's drug use began to take a hold of the young actor. The first reports of drug-taking on film sets came during the making of *My Own Private Idaho*. 'I've copped back some weird earplay about me and acid,' Phoenix said at the time. 'I just thought it was a joke. I thought they weren't being serious. I thought it was this reverse psychology trying to get information out of someone - "I heard you took acid". I would just laugh. It would frighten the hell out of me to be a creature walking around in the nineties taking acid.'

Phoenix continued: 'Acid doesn't really supply you with any answers. My best friends since I was eight were older people, and I've heard every acid trip in the world. And I've been there. I've really been totally, completely able to understand the experience to the point where I've been stimulated vicariously. The thing is, right now, why throw a curve on life?...I tell ya what. That's actually not such a bad rumour to have going around about you....' Maybe having an untrue rumour about taking acid was better than admitting what he was really doing.

'There were rumours of people using heroin on that movie,' confirmed Mickey Cottrell, publicist for *My Own Private Idaho*, 'But I was there and I didn't see anything.' However, the shooting conditions of *My Own Private Idaho* were ripe for it. Ralph Rugoff, writing in *Premiere* magazine reported: 'Having recently bought a large Victorian house, [Van Sant] invited several of the street kids in the cast to use it as a crash pad. Phoenix and Reeves moved in shortly afterward, and the place soon took on the aspect of a rock'n'roll dormitory, with futons spread out on the floor and guitar jam sessions lasting through the night. Van Sant, in need of time alone, ended up retreating to a downtown loft.'

It isn't impossible that living in that atmosphere, among a mix of professional actors, street kids who were playing bit parts in the movie and rock'n'rollers like Flea, that Phoenix could have been tempted by drugs - the major Hollywood vice that he'd always spoken out against. One of the other actors on the film spoke about the drug scene during the production of the film to *Spin* Magazine. 'Everyone was getting high. It was the nature of the film. Some of these guys had been through this before, and as soon as filming was over, they gave it up and got back to their work. This was the first time for River, though, and he just went wild.' And he wasn't mature enough to leave it and go back to his clean life. But you can be sure that he didn't expect it to kill him.'

William Richert probably knew Phoenix better than anyone else on *My*

Own Private Idaho, the two having worked together before on *A Night in the Life of Jimmy Reardon*. 'I heard a lot of rumours,' said Richert of the drugs allegations, '[that] he's doing this controversial stuff, mixed up with real junkies. River had this kind of out-of-it personality. He was in almost every scene and we were shooting from six in the morning till eleven at night, because there was no money. I can't imagine he could have been doing very much playing that part; I just can't understand how, physically, one could do that.'

Gus Van Sant denied being aware of Phoenix using drugs during production of the film. 'I never saw any instance of that on set. But you never know.' After the actor's death, Van Sant was quick to praise him. 'River was one of the most amazing people that ever lived; he reminded me of Bobby Kennedy. It didn't seem to me that there was some kind of hidden problem. River was extremely artistic, and there must be some pain in there somewhere. But I don't think it was the wrong kind of pain.'

After Phoenix's death, Ronald Bergan, in an obituary for *The Guardian*, reported: 'Around that time [the making of *My Own Private Idaho*], River had been tempted to take drugs. Earlier, he had claimed: "I've never been offered drugs on set, but it has happened to friends of mine. Actors who use them will ask a kid if he wants some."'

River Phoenix was well aware of the problems of his *Stand By Me* co-star Corey Feldman, who'd had his fair share of trouble growing up in public in Hollywood since appearing alongside Phoenix in the Rob Reiner movie in 1986. Alcohol and drug abuse were only two of them, leading to an arrest in 1989 by the police on drugs charges. At the time that Feldman's problems were hitting the headlines, Phoenix had commented: 'It makes you realise drugs aren't just done by bad guys and sleazebags; it's a universal disease.'

Feldman felt lucky to be caught. He went through the process of becoming 'clean', rebuilding his life and career. Feldman had also heard the stories about his friend Phoenix and drug taking: 'I heard that during the filming of *My Own Private Idaho*, River was doing heroin. Then watching clips from the film and looking at the pictures and interviews with him, and the way he was talking and the way he was acting, I presumed it to be true.'

Feldman made serious attempts to help his one time co-star to begin to address what was clearly becoming a serious problem. 'I thought maybe he could take a hint. I basically said: "My life is great. I've gotten clean. I'm doing wonderful, how're you doing?" And he was in a lot of denial and said "I'm fine, everything's fine". That kind of thing.'

Feldman left it at that, but received a call from Phoenix about a week later. 'I believe it was his way of seeking help. He left a message saying "Please call me back as soon as you can." By the time I did, he was back in denial. But I believe there was a brief moment when maybe something I said had affected him.'

River Phoenix (centre) with his band, Aleka's Attic. It featured his sister Rain (top right).

Chapter 8

A S WELL as his vegetarianism, pro-healthy living and anti-fur stance, River Phoenix was well known in Hollywood and beyond for having spoken out strongly at one time against drug use. 'You don't even have to seek it out,' he had said. 'It finds you. In the dressing room or the make-up trailer, someone will say "If you don't tell anyone, I'll let you try some." It's so accessible and so stylish. I hate all that.'

It seems to have been a short step for Phoenix from being aware of the problem - and warning against it - to finding himself in circumstances when it was hard to resist the temptation to join in with what everyone else was doing. He carried forward from filming on *My Own Private Idaho* more of the character of Mike than he had of any previous part he played. Since that film wrapped production, Phoenix had become an occasional, but habitual, user of drugs.

Drugs are a big part of the LA club scene. Phoenix had gone from being a film star VIP guest in the secluded back rooms of the more exclusive clubs to playing guitar up on stage and acting like a rock star. It's little wonder he found himself involved in the drug scene he had previously managed to avoid in the film world. His concentration on Aleka's Attic and the posing in the 'underground' world of rock was ultimately to lead to his downfall.

'He may have been a vegetarian, but that doesn't mean he didn't use drugs,' an anonymous Hollywood source told *The Washington Post* after Phoenix's death, further claiming that Phoenix had been seen using drugs on the sets of several films in the year before his death.

The story of Phoenix's dabbling in drugs may go further back than this, according to the claims of one Rick Riojas, reported by *The Star* in New York. After the actor's death, Riojas claimed to be Phoenix's drug supplier. 'I was with River [in 1989] the first time he used heroin, and he couldn't "shoot" himself. So I grabbed his arm, stuck the needle in a good vein and pushed the plunger.'

River Phoenix had deeply-held convictions about the
natural world and continued to campaign on
environmental issues to the end of his life.

The result of that 'good deed' by Riojas was, according to *The Star*, a $1000 a week cocaine and heroin addiction. *The Star* reported that Riojas claimed: 'He was loaded all the time. [One weekend] I sold out and even my connection sold out [to Phoenix].' From that first experience in 1989, it seems that Phoenix's film experiences on *My Own Private Idaho* and moves in the world of rock'n'roll only served to reinforce the temptations. According to a nameless friend of the actor talking to *The Enquirer*, Phoenix had been using drugs infrequently from about 1989-90. 'I saw River using heroin and cocaine on several occasions.'

It was early in 1993, according to Riojas, that Phoenix became interested in mixing drugs and asked Riojas if he'd ever tried 'speedballs', a cocaine and heroin combination nicknamed Belushis, after the one which killed comic actor John Belushi in the Chateau Marmont Motel in 1982.

Belushi had come to fame on the late night TV show *Saturday Night Live*, alongside Chevy Chase and Dan Aykroyd. Graduating to a series of films, including *Animal House* (1978) and *The Blues Brothers* (1980, with Aykroyd), Belushi had found his more mainstream acting ambitions thwarted. He was notorious for his hard living and reckless drug taking. On 5th March1982 Belushi had died from a drug overdose after being injected by his friend Cathy Smith. Belushi had taken a 'speedball', a mixture of cocaine and heroin, although the final cause of death was attributed to a toxic build up of drugs over several days leading to respiratory failure. Belushi missed out on a major part in *Ghostbusters* (1984), which had been written especially for him (Bill Murray took the role) and Cathy Smith was indicted for murder.

The case shocked Hollywood and led to a major public clean up of the image attached to Tinseltown as the eighties began. But, while 'Just Say No', Nancy Reagan's anti-drugs slogan, was the public preaching of Hollywood, behind the scenes things went on much as before. Again, according to *The Star*, Riojas claimed he'd last seen Phoenix in the summer of 1993. Phoenix reportedly told Riojas: 'Dude, you were right. John Belushis are the ultimate high.'

Speaking to *The Enquirer*, an anonymous friend of the actor relayed River Phoenix's justification for his growing drug taking: 'He told me "Life's too short not to live it up. I don't want to die from old age in a nursing home - I'll be the best looking guy in the morgue!"'

There are other accounts of Phoenix's increasingly reckless approach to drugs throughout 1993. After Phoenix's death, columnist Taki reported in *The Spectator* on 13th November 1993 that the actor's drugs-related death had come as no surprise to him. 'Early this year,' he claimed, 'an actress friend of mine living in the palm-lined Sodom [LA] had told me a ghastly story about Phoenix's compulsive drug-taking. He was in her house, high on cocaine and GHB, a form of Ecstasy but much, much stronger, and was popping

*River Phoenix as James Wright in Peter Bogdanovich's
The Thing Called Love. River wrote a song for the movie
called 'Lone Star State of Mind'.*

morphine tablets to come down. My friend told me River almost died in her house that very night in January, so when I read how everyone thought he was clean until it happened, I laughed out loud.'

Similarly, others reported seeing Phoenix high on drugs at public occasions. 'I saw him in May or June at the USA Film Festival in Dallas. You couldn't even talk to him he was so stoned,' an anonymous source commented to *People* Magazine.

Before his death River Phoenix had completed two films and was working on a third. The first completed and given a limited theatrical release in the United States was Peter Bogdanovich's *The Thing Called Love* (1993). It is the tale of four friends on the verge of making a breakthrough as Country and Western musicians. They have travelled to Nashville in search of fame and fortune, or at the very least a record deal. Phoenix plays James Wright, a guitar wielding cowboy who is out to win the heart of Miranda (Samantha Mathis) away from her boyfriend Kyle (Dermot Mulroney, who was also to co-star in Phoenix's next project *Silent Tongue*).

Also in the cast is Sandra Bullock and *The Thing Called Love* featured the debut film performances from Country music stars Trisha Yearwood, playing herself, and K. T. Oslin, playing a 'den mother' to the new breed of amateur performers hanging around the Bluebird Cafe.

Phoenix was partly attracted to the film because of its musical emphasis - although Country and Western music is very far removed from the progressive rock of Aleka's Attic. However, the film did give him a chance to indulge his musical talents on screen, as it called for the actors to not only sing but also play their own instruments. 'I'm totally into Country music,' said Phoenix on the set of *The Thing Called Love*, 'because of its root form. But I'm not doing this film to get recognition for my music.' He was hesitant about featuring his singing or music in a film role, however. 'I always felt that music and singing was something of a hobby and never intended to portray a character that would perform in this way, but there was a reality I could bring to this role that was vital.'

Despite that claim, Phoenix did write a song entitled *Lone Star State of Mind* specifically for the film and he got several chances to play live and sing, showing exactly what he could do. 'The song is an ode to solitude and the preservation of one's independence,' said Phoenix of *Lone Star State of Mind*.

Director Peter Bogdanovich came to *The Thing Called Love* after years of unsuccessful projects following his early film success in the late sixties and early seventies, such as *Targets* (1967) and *The Last Picture Show* (1971). 'It wasn't a big leap for me to see River in this role,' he said. 'With a name like that don't you think he sounds a little like a Country singer?' The idea of casting Phoenix obviously struck a chord with Paramount executives, since they had previously refused to give the go-ahead to a project that required

the stars to do their own singing.

In some respects, Phoenix found himself returning to themes treated in *A Night in the Life of Jimmy Reardon*, but this time with no teen comedy/romance angle. 'Orson Welles once said there are two things that are virtually impossible to do well in the movies,' said Bogdanovich. 'That's prayer and sex. This gets pretty sexy, but there's no flesh to speak of. It's not like you get to see their...I think the actors wanted it to be a little more torrid than it is. You do get to see them kiss - and it's a very good kiss.'

Phoenix described his character in the film as a 'self-centred, narcissistic musician' who is trying to start a romance with Samantha Mathis. Phoenix met Mathis for the first time on the set of *The Thing Called Love* and soon began a relationship with her. He was spending less and less time in Gainesville and this had caused inevitable strains on his relationship with Sue Solgot who remained behind in Florida. 'He was crazy about [Samantha Mathis] right away', said Peter Bogdanovich. 'He was anxious to have lots of

A scene from The Thing Called Love: River Phoenix (standing) with co-stars Dermot Mulroney and Samantha Mathis.

kissing scenes. He was saying, "In the lovemaking scene, can we really do it? Can you just put us in there, close the door and let us go?" He was only half-kidding.'

This new relationship with Mathis did not prevent several reports of drugged and difficult behaviour from River Phoenix on the set. One crew member on the film commented: 'He acted messed up and confused and he seemed real thin and unhealthy.' His behind-the-scenes reputation for drug abuse on location in Tennessee was said to be so serious that one night's filming featuring Phoenix was reportedly unusable.

From the set of *The Thing Called Love* Phoenix gave a somewhat incoherent interview to Tom Daniels of the British newspaper *The Mail on Sunday*, which was published after the actor's death. Daniels described Phoenix as having a pallid complexion, with dirty brown hair, looking like a 23 year old 'who had been up all night'.

Phoenix spoke of his desire for a big box office hit to enable him to continue to do the off beat and independent work that he preferred. 'I need to get up there with the big box office types. Well, not necessarily, but it would help a great deal. You must have the conventional success to have the unconventional success. If I can do two independent films a year and one corporate monster film like this a year, three in total, then I'll be happy.'

'I've learnt an awful lot on this shoot for *The Thing Called Love* - this is my college. I've worked my butt off for this,' said Phoenix of the film, which was

*River Phoenix and Dermot Mulroney in The Thing Called
Love. They were to co-star again in Sam Shepard's Silent
Tongue, River's last completed film*

subject to a luke warm critical reception. 'If this film doesn't work, it's someone else's fault. I would like to make films where it's all my fault. But that's
not my place. I'm just doing my job and it's someone else's fault then.'

Phoenix seemed to be worried about the quality of the film he was
involved in and even with his own performance. He was resigned to the fact
that the film would by-pass cinemas and be released straight onto home
video. 'It'll be out there for ever. So I suppose I have no regrets, ultimately,'
he said.

A large part of the interview focused on the confusion that Phoenix suffered at the hands of director Bogdanovich, who had him shoot three different versions of a simple scene featuring a dog, but with three different
emotional reactions and three different back stories for the dog. This would
normally have been simple, if tedious, work for an actor of Phoenix's ability,
but in the interview with Daniels, he seems to admit to having found this rel-
atively simple filmic task difficult to comprehend. 'Having to do something
like that changes your reactions. Somebody talks about a dog - either I had a
dog that was hit or the other variation was I still had a dog that my dad left
me when he died. I had three different things to play.'

'I don't think I'm a very good actor,' Phoenix admitted, his old doubts
raising their heads again. Now his doubts were more related to his ability to
act *and* maintain his by now constant drug intake, without it being discovered and everything falling apart. 'Everything is kind of tentative and at a

*River Phoenix with Samantha Mathis in The Thing Called Love.
She became his real-life girlfriend and was with him on the night
that he died.*

certain point you just feel the Holy Ghost move you. It's a great feeling. It's not like I reason and say "Oh, I want to do this", it's just like an inherent challenge that grips you and says, "Do it!". Your subconscious says go with it, make it something. I think I can root out characters pretty well. I can be possessed pretty well.'

Phoenix seemed confused about his commitment to his work, about trying to carve out a further direction for his career. 'I learned that to try and play God with your life will wreck your brain and your nervous system, and mess up your natural direction in the course that's already there. I just don't want to read about me being made a basket case because of my work. It's self-pity that I hate. I mean, it comes with the territory. An actor with any conviction goes the extra mile - but of course you're gonna suffer damage to your brain. The point is not to lose yourself completely. I'm working on giving more.'

Considering the reports from the set of *The Thing Called Love* the finished film is a surprisingly coherent and entertaining journey into the lives of wannabe Country and Western singer-songwriters. Phoenix is at his best on stage during the musical numbers: *The Thing Called Love* was the only film in his career that really gave him the chance to display his musical talents. It's just as well that he got to do so, as the rest of his performance is extremely poor, given his previously evident talent.

Phoenix claimed he was getting deep into the character, but the incoherent mumbling and methody-acting posing that passes for his performance are clear signs of an actor who had, at least for the moment, passed his creative peak. What remains in the film shows a serious-minded actor who has seriously lost his way – the material left on the cutting room floor is even more revealing.

Peter Bogdanovich seems to have realised that Phoenix had problems and expressed worries about them. He described how he tackled River when the actor became moody and withdrawn: "I took him aside and said, "Are you on something?" He said no. I said, "Well, you're acting kind of strange and Sam's upset." He said, "Oh, Jesus, I'm just – this is a difficult character. I'm into this part and I'm just trying to deal with where he's at at this point. Jeez, I'm sorry. I don't mean to upset Sam." I said, "I don't want any getting into drugs. We don't need that." And he said, "No, no, man". He said, "I took a decongestant and half a beer and maybe that was a mistake. But I'm fine, I'm okay now."'

It was not the only time that Bogdanovich had cause to raise the topic of drugs with Phoenix. 'I alluded to rumours I'd heard. I wanted to see what he'd say. There were some rumours that he was on drugs on our picture, which angered me, because it was impossible. I know how the rumour got started. We were kind of rewriting the script as we went along, and it was difficult to know how far to take the weirdness of the character. We might do twelve takes or more of a given scene, and each one would be different. He had complete control over it. If he was on drugs he wouldn't have been able to control it. But some of the people at the studio, seeing some of the footage, said, "Oh, he must be on drugs."'

'It's like feeling like the invisible man,' Phoenix had said of Los Angeles and the dangers of living there. 'You start disintegrating, you can't see yourself and you feel like you're being absorbed into this big blob of glitter.' In an attempt to cover up, Phoenix was reportedly attending Alcoholics Anonymous meetings in LA and he often worked out in a gym with his own personal trainer in a futile attempt to hide the tell tale physical signs of heavy drug abuse. Anthony Clark, who also starred in *The Thing Called Love*, was aware that all was not right with the actor during the making of the film. "I feel really bad, because I felt like he was there for everybody, and nobody was there for him. I knew maybe there were problems with...I didn't know what...I was scared to ask, because a few times I did talk to him about his intense situations with alcohol. I brought it up, but he was such a great actor that he would just totally calm my nerves...I wish to God that I could have stepped in and intervened, but he just seemed so incredibly together."

After his death, Naomi Foner, scriptwriter for *Running On Empty*, felt that what Phoenix needed at this stage of his life was a shock to wake him up to the increasingly desperate reality of his situation: 'I think the best thing that could have happened to River is that somebody fired him off a film. If he was working drugged, he should have been told "There are limits here." But I think he was a good enough actor probably to con his way out of these situations.'

Phoenix's drug addiction remained the worst kept secret in Hollywood. The public didn't know about it and continued to believe that Phoenix was some kind of nature boy saint. However, the talk of the town was of the increasing numbers of appearances in public where Phoenix was clearly on something. Nevertheless, he continued to work as he was still a respected figure in the industry. He still managed to secure roles on challenging films and work with challenging directors, the latest being Sam Shepard on the film *Silent Tongue* (1993).

When Talbot Roe's (River Phoenix) half-indian wife Awbonnie (Sheila Tousey) dies in childbirth, he becomes crazed with grief and sits in lonely vigil in the middle of a desolate prairie, guarding her body in a burial tree. In order to save his son from going completely mad, Prescott Roe (Richard Harris) gallops across the vast prairie in search of Eamon MacCree (Alan Bates), who runs the Kickapoo Indian Medicine Show, and who traded him Awbonnie for horses. Prescott intends to buy Eamon's second daughter, Velada (Jeri Arredondo), who is the medicine show's trick rider. He believes that only

*The fragility of River's personality became increasingly
apparent towards the end of 1993.*

she can save Talbot from his terrible grief.

Eamon is willing to consider the deal until his son Reeves (Dermot Mulroney) violently objects, forcing a delay in the trade. Unable to wait, Prescott kidnaps Velada and heads back across the plains to the burial tree and his grief stricken son, Talbot.

Back at the tree, Awbonnie's ghost - a powerful and terrible presence - rises from her body and demands that Talbot let the animals devour her body and free her to enter the spirit world. In his grief, Talbot refuses, throwing the ghost into a fearsome rage. She demands her release with the righteous anger of a Kiowa warrior and also wants justice for the girls' mother, the woman they call Silent Tongue (Tantoo Cardinal), who had been raped years before by a white man who fathered her two mixed-blood daughters, Awbonnie and Velada.

Sam Shepard built his reputation as a great American playwright and actor. *Far North* (1988) was Shepard's film directing debut, leaving behind some of the complications of his plays for a fairly straightforward approach to this tale of a crumbling Minnesota farm family. *Silent Tongue* was only his second attempt at film making, which he shot near Roswell, New Mexico. This meticulously researched and well told story brought both the director and River Phoenix some very positive reviews.

Geoffrey Gilmore, writing about the film for the programme book of the Sundance Film Festival wrote: 'Shepard's accomplishment is no less than a redefinition of the Western. The drama is distinctive and multi-levelled, and the legacy of the Native American is emphatically recalled and realised. This is a film with a personal and ideological vision and the power to influence our sense of both the past and the future.' Gilmore also felt that *Silent Tongue* featured 'superb performances from a standout cast'.

It was to be the final film that River Phoenix would complete.

Chapter 9

THE LAST film that River Phoenix worked on was *Dark Blood* (1993). The $8 million thriller was to tell the story of two city dwellers, played by Jonathan Pryce and Judy Davis, who have an encounter with an alternately charming and terrifying character called only Boy, played by River Phoenix.

Dutch film director George Sluizer had come to prominence following his 1988 chiller *Spoorloos (The Vanishing)*. The film, which told of a man's obsessive search for his kidnapped girlfriend, was an art-house hit all over Europe and drew Sluizer - who had been working independently in Europe for 35 years - to the attention of the Hollywood studios. Offered a budget of $20 million to remake *The Vanishing* as an American movie in English, Sluizer was happy to accept a deal which increased his budget ten times over the original and gave him a way into the American film industry.

The new film cast Kiefer Sutherland as the boyfriend and Jeff Bridges as the kidnapper, and is a far more straightforward and hence less interesting version of the story. However, Sluizer realised that having completed *The Vanishing* successfully, he could then go on to make some of his own projects in America. *Dark Blood* was to be the first, he hoped, of many.

The production of *Dark Blood* was not a happy experience for many of those involved, not only River Phoenix who was continuing to struggle with his growing drug and alcohol problem. Actress Judy Davis was having a hard time with director George Sluizer, and she claimed that the director was also the source of Phoenix's problems with his role. 'He was having troubles with his character...It was a difficult part, because it could so easily be absurd. He had most of the dialogue in the film, huge speeches; he kept trying to cut the lines down. Any change freaked the director out.'

The feeling that all was not right on the set of *Dark Blood* reached everyone. Jonathan Pryce recalled premonitions of disaster during the filming: 'River said, "Somebody's going to die on this film". We were on this kind of

Photographers such as Nancy Ellison found River
Phoenix's vulnerable good looks an irresistible subject.

inexorable journey to some disaster. Every day there was some kind of difficulty. It just seemed as if something had to give.'

For the six weeks immediately before his death River Phoenix had been 300 miles south of Salt Lake City, near a town called Torrey on location for *Dark Blood*. Phoenix was interviewed on location for *Dark Blood* for the last time by a group of journalists, including Jean-Paul Chaillet of French *Premiere* magazine. 'He was extremely polite,' said Chaillet of Phoenix, 'considerate, looking you in the eye.' Phoenix, to the end, was still discussing topics that concerned him, such as the plight of Native Americans and the backwards step of resumption of nuclear testing by the United States. Some people noted that Phoenix appeared thin and ill at ease at times.

Certainly Phoenix was not happy on the location for *Dark Blood* – whether it was his difficulty with the part or some of his larger problems that got to him, no-one will ever know. River seemed to be seriously considering whether he had any long term future in the acting business, whether he could continue to make films and not succumb totally to the temptations his lifestyle placed before him. William Richert had received a message from Phoenix on his answering machine: 'The last time I heard from him he said, "I'm out here in Utah and I'm having a kind of hard time keeping my head above water in this crazy business".'

As with his most recent films, allegations of drug use on film sets followed Phoenix to *Dark Blood*, although director George Sluizer had no doubts in his mind on this issue. 'He did not use anything during the period we were in Utah.' Judy Davis had formed a different opinion: 'I thought he was doing something when I first got there. There was one day when he came in so out of it.'

Phoenix had finished location filming for *Dark Blood* and had returned to Los Angeles at the end of October. The film company had booked a suite at the Nikko hotel on La Cienega Boulevard, a large Japanese-owned business hotel. Having worked on studio scenes for *Dark Blood* during the day on Saturday 30th October 1993, Phoenix had Sunday 31st - Halloween - off, so was intending to relax, to be a rock star rather than an actor.

Those involved recalled the last day that Phoenix shot on *Dark Blood* vividly. 'The scene that we were doing on Saturday - we were both supposed to be on peyote,' said Judy Davis. 'I had had a conversation with him a few weeks before, saying that I wouldn't take peyote just to see what it's like in order to play the scene. I recall River agreeing with me about that. We didn't work on Friday. We had just come back to LA. I think he'd driven out with all his friends and they'd let their hair down. He took, I think, Valium to bring himself down, and that's where the problems started...'

George Sluizer agreed that during the day on Saturday was when things began to go seriously wrong for Phoenix. He'd escaped the pressures of filming on location in Utah, and although many of the fim's major scenes were still to be shot, it would be under the more controlled conditions of a studio set. Sluizer said: 'On Saturday - well, this is my own personal feeling - he had taken something. The last day, I had a feeling that he was a little, let's say, nebulous. He was a bit like someone who had slept for two hours instead of seven.'

The director of photography on *Dark Blood*, Ed Lachman, recalled clearly the final scenes shot featuring River Phoenix: 'We did ten takes of the soliloquy, the last day we shot with him on *Dark Blood*. It was in this cave, could have been a church. It was all lit by candles. After the last take, I didn't turn the camera off. When I realised it was still running, I turned it off. When we saw dailies, for ten seconds River was in front of the camera, just a silhouette lit by ambient light. It was...eerie...People were crying. We knew that was the last we would see of River.'

That evening Phoenix had some friends come around to the hotel and ordered food and drinks when they arrived. Room service delivered the food and drink, noting the loud music and chaotic state of the room, as well as the allegedly spaced out expression on River Phoenix's face. At 10.30pm Phoenix called the front desk and asked for his car to be brought round to the front of the hotel. There were reports of a commotion among the Phoenix party as they left the Nikko, heading for The Viper Room. Phoenix slumped in the back of the car while one of the others drove.

The Viper Room is a night club, co-owned by movie actor Johnny Depp and rock star Chuck E. Weiss situated on the corner of Larrabee Street and the stretch of Sunset Boulevard known as Sunset Strip in Los Angeles. It was outside The Viper Room that River Phoenix was to give his final public performance.

When he took it over, Depp had The Viper Room remodelled to resemble a vintage Hollywood speakeasy - dimly lit, with much art-deco decoration and a corner stage where Depp and his musician friends could perform. The new-look club opened in August 1993, the latest addition to the Sunset Strip club scene.

The Viper Room has a capacity of just 200 people, but no sooner had it opened than it built up a roster of star name regulars that included *Beverly Hills 90210* TV star Shannen Doherty, Tori Spelling, Christina Applegate and Red Hot Chilli Pepper bassist Flea. River Phoenix was also a regular when in LA on film work, either to play with Aleka's Attic on stage, or just to hang out among the musicians.

Drugs are an accepted fact of life on the Westside and Sunset Strip club circuit, frequented by many of the younger stars of Hollywood and the rock world - the very circles that River Phoenix had been moving in since 1989-90.

They are easily bought and usually discreetly taken. Many of the trendy clubs boast hidden back rooms for the privileged few, those who are flavour of the month, 'in' at the moment. In these back rooms, drugs can be taken and shared in relative privacy. The Viper Room was no exception.

The drugs taken range from the most easily available, Ecstasy ('E' - a synthetic hallucinogenic amphetamine), cocaine and more fashionably than ever in the early nineties, heroin. Marijuana had undergone something of a revival too with the young, affluent crowd who frequent the likes of the Viper Room, the Whisky-a-Go-Go and Oscars.

Newly introduced on the club drug scene was a so-called 'designer' drug, GHB - gamma hydroxybutyrate acid, a synthetic steroid that induces feelings of euphoria and relaxation. GHB had moved from the body building world to the club circuit, only to become the latest trendy drug to be seen taking. It was considered a very convenient drug, too, coming in powder or capsule form, which was usually boiled into a liquid by users. It's known with cynical irony among club goers as GBH.

GHB first came to public notice when British rock star Billy Idol collapsed with convulsions outside a trendy Beverly Hills club called Tatou. Idol was rushed to hospital and soon recovered from a condition that his publicist attributed to 'exhaustion'. Press reports recounted people close to Idol who claimed he was actually suffering from a GHB overdose.

Until 1990, the drug was publicly promoted in health food stores and was easily available by mail order as a legal psychedelic and a weight loss aid. However, by the early 90s, the Federal Drug Administration had linked over 30 cases of illness in California, Georgia and Florida to GHB abuse. Despite this evidence, the drug quickly caught on in the Hollywood club circuit.

Regulars at The Viper Room were well aware that a great variety of drugs were available and were being consumed on the premises. The back room, frequented by celebrities, was jokingly known as The Smack Room. It was to The Viper Room that River Phoenix was to make his way on the night of Saturday 30th October 1993.

Arriving at around 11.30pm Phoenix met up with his girlfriend of the moment, actress Samantha Mathis, his actor-brother Leaf (Joaquin), and other friends, including Red Hot Chilli Pepper's Flea. An anonymous source, quoted by *National Enquirer*, claimed that Phoenix 'was already out of it on drugs when he got to the club'.

The Phoenix party sat at a table by the small dance floor and ordered up drinks. Another source who was in the club that evening - again unnamed - claimed that Phoenix 'just looked completely stoned. It was quite apparent that he was on something. He was table hopping and bumping into tables.'

Willing to speak on the record of the events of 30th October in The Viper Room was Heather McDougal, a Viper Room regular since August. 'I got here about 11.45,' she told Ian Parker, writing in the British newspaper *The Independent on Sunday*. 'It was a completely different crowd than usual, a lot of heavy-core rocker types. It was a very weird feeling.' McDougal had missed her date, whom she was supposed to be meeting at the club, but she did notice River Phoenix. 'Standing over there, by the mirror, with some people, hanging out, having a good time. He didn't look abnormal. People say "Oh, he was acting weird", because they want it to be that way...' But Phoenix was reported to have been 'acting strangely' that evening, by among others, his brother Leaf.

Various eyewitness accounts claim that Phoenix may have been drinking copious quantities of a potent German herbal-based liqueur called Jagermeister. One report had Phoenix disappearing to the back room of The Viper Room and injecting himself with a heroin-cocaine 'speedball'. However, the autopsy report of 15th November indicated no needle marks on the actor's body, concluding that the drugs taken had been 'ingested or inhaled'. One club goer claimed that liquid GHB was being passed around in The Viper Room that evening, and that it was not unknown for drinks to be spiked with drugs without the drinker knowing anything about it until the drugs begin to take effect. In a special report on 'Drugs and Young Hollywood', *Entertainment Weekly* on 26th November highlighted private parties at which, according to one party goer, 'They put ecstasy in the punch.'

At one stage during the evening, Phoenix was said to have become hyperactive, careening around the club, with little regard for his own personal safety or that of anyone else. He was due to join Johnny Depp on stage at the end of the evening for a jam session. Having calmed down, Phoenix was back behind his table with his friends, when he began to vomit on himself. Taken to the washroom, he began to shudder violently in front of the sink, while concerned club-goers doused him with water. It was now about 1.00am on Sunday 31st October 1993; Halloween.

Returning to his table, the seizures began again, and Phoenix slipped under the table. At this point, he was taken outside, apparently at the request of Johnny Depp, who was jamming on stage with Flea, Gibby Haynes of the Butthole Surfers and Al Jorgensen of Ministry. Depp had only met River Phoenix once before that evening. On his way out of The Viper Room, River Phoenix is alleged to have called out to Depp on the corner stage: 'I'm gonna die, dude!'

Heather McDougal had gone out from The Viper Room earlier in the evening to get air and came back to a commotion on the sidewalk outside the club: 'There was an ambulance, a cop car. I stopped a guy and said "What's happening?". He said "Someone's not feeling well." And then I saw - they were loading him onto the ambulance. He was dead.'

Photographer Ron Davis, who had been trawling Sunset Strip for celebrity photographs around club land on the evening of the 30th and on the early morning of the 31st had arrived at The Viper Room as the final call of the evening. Davis had been to Tatou, Babylon, Spago, and the Dome, among other star-attracting venues and had managed to take a couple of personality photos. He arrived at The Viper Room just in time to witness River Phoenix's last moments. Unusual among the so-called paparazzi, Davis seeks permission of those celebrities he photographs and took no pictures of the events concerning River Phoenix outside The Viper Room.

Waiting outside while Halloween revellers passed by, Davis claims that shortly after 1am the club door opened and River Phoenix was carried out, held between Samantha Mathis, who Davis recognised, and his brother Leaf. Rain followed, along with Christina Applegate, an actress in the TV series *Married...with Children*.

At first Davis didn't recognise that the man being carried out of the club - whom he assumed to be drunk - was the actor River Phoenix. For his role in *Dark Blood* Phoenix had had his hair dyed black and he was wearing jeans and black Converse sneakers.

On this night, of all nights, such a ghoulish display as that which unfolded on the pavement outside The Viper Room was regarded as nothing terribly unusual. 'It looked,' said Sean Tuttle, manager of the Whisky A Go Go across the street, 'like a normal occurrence.' People passing by veered clear around the man convulsing on the sidewalk and the group of friends who surrounded him.

According to Davis, when Phoenix first hit the ground, the doorman of The Viper Room 'was saying "Do something, call 911!" The brother [Leaf] kept looking back at him and yelling "He's fine, he's fine, he's fine."'

Phoenix suffered further seizures on the sidewalk. 'His eyes were all back in his head, rolled back beyond his eye lids,' said Davis. 'He was shaking and his arms were flailing around.' The similarity with his on-screen simulated seizure at the end of *My Own Private Idaho* was chilling.

By now, Leaf had rushed to a nearby pay phone to call for paramedics on 911. In an anguished plea for help that was to be played and replayed on the news nightly for days following Phoenix's death, Leaf was heard to say: 'You must get here, please, you must get here. I'm thinking he had valium or something.'

'He looked like a fish out of water,' said Davis of Phoenix at this stage, '...flapping around the sidewalk like a guppy.'

With his head banging on the pavement Rain attempted to lay on top of her dying brother to try and still his spasms. Following a fifth and final seizure there was stillness. On the payphone, Leaf told the 911 operator,

'He's not having seizures any more. He's just passed out...He just looks like he's sleeping.'

'After eight minutes of seizure, arms flopping, his knuckles hitting the sidewalk, his feet flopping up and down, after about eight minutes of that he finally became still, completely still,' said Davis. Rain lay on the pavement next to her brother. Ron Davis recalled: 'She lifted up his shirt and was rubbing his tummy and saying "Can you hear me? Can you hear me...?"'

The paramedic team arrived within minutes of Leaf's frantic phone call and about five minutes after Phoenix's final seizure. Fire Captain Raymond Ribar headed the four strong team of medics and made an on-the-spot diagnosis of the problem he was dealing with: 'It was the classic cocaine overreaction - it just nails some people and stops the heart,' he said.

The paramedics tried to revive Phoenix, giving basic life support on the sidewalk. Only now did a curious crowd form, witnesses to River Phoenix's last performance. As Phoenix was lifted into an ambulance Michael Balzary (Flea) joined the group and got into the front of the ambulance for the short journey to the Cedars-Sinai Medical Center. Leaf and Depp also made their way to the emergency room, a few blocks south of The Viper Room.

It was 1.34am when River Phoenix arrived in the hospital, in full cardiac arrest. Blood samples taken at the time, as surgeons opened his chest in an attempt to restart the heart, indicated valium and cocaine in high, certainly toxic, levels. River Phoenix was pronounced dead at 1.51am, after 20 minutes in the emergency room, on Sunday 31st October 1993.

While the Phoenix family closed ranks, releasing a statement that 'his beauty, gentleness, compassion, vulnerability and love is a gift for all eternity', a preliminary autopsy on River Phoenix's body was held on Monday 1st November, as speculation mounted that his death was somehow, shockingly, drug-related. Could it really be true that the 23-year-old actor who proclaimed the benefits of a 'clean' lifestyle, who had spoken out on so many topics, from fur to rain forests, had succumbed to the scourge of Hollywood - drugs? And that despite the best efforts of his parents and agents, who were only too aware of the temptations that lay in store for a successful, rich, young star in LA?

The media had a field day in the weeks after his death. Here was a new James Dean, although as often as Dean was mentioned by newspaper obituary writers and TV commentators alike, so too was the far less glamorous name of John Belushi. Conclusive toxicology reports were released on 12th November, with the media world-wide reporting the results. Coroner spokesman Scott Carrier blamed Phoenix's death on 'acute multiple drug intoxications'. The Coroner concluded drugs had been 'ingested or inhaled' as no obvious needle marks had been found on the body of the actor, sug-

gesting that if he had a recent history of drug abuse, he had not been injecting. The toxicology tests had shown high levels of cocaine and morphine in
Phoenix's blood stream. (Upon absorption into the blood stream, through
chemical processes heroin becomes morphine.)

Coroner's spokesman Scott Carrier concluded: 'The manner of death is
ruled as accidental.' In all, the post mortem, officially held on 15th November, showed traces of marijuana and valium, morphine, cocaine, and cold
medication - but no alcohol. Carrier noted that additional toxicology tests
were to be carried out to detect the presence of GHB.

Detectives had been called in to investigate the possibility of foul play.
LA Deputy Bill Martin felt the investigation was warranted as 'it is unusual
for someone of that age to die like this. He was in the prime of his life.' However, the results of the toxicology tests ended the criminal investigation, with
the 'accidental death' ruling precluding any possible criminal proceedings.
In the early 1980s, the LA Police Department had operated an Entertain-
ments Squad within its drug division, aimed at investigating illegal drug use
in the show business community. This had been disbanded in 1984, however, as the pressing problems of the growth of drug abuse in inner city poorer
neighbourhoods cut into Police Department resources. Hence the fact that
much of the club scene in and around Sunset Strip where drugs were readily
available was beyond the reach of the law. Several months before Phoenix's
death, however, Dave Valentine of LA County Sheriff's Department, had
stepped up efforts to mount an ongoing investigation of the club scene, particularly in the light of the spread of GHB use. Valentine had found monitor-
ing the exclusive night-spots an 'uphill struggle', according to *Entertainment
Weekly*. 'The drug scene up there is a lot worse over the past few years. It's
gone from cocaine, marijuana, heroin into designer things. I'm no longer sur-
prised at how many famous people use [drugs],' he said, following
Phoenix's death.

The Viper Room was closed immediately following River Phoenix's death. A
notice outside read: 'With much respect and love to River and his family, The
Viper Room is temporarily closed. Our heartfelt condolences to all his family, friends and loved ones. He will be missed. - All of us at The Viper Room.'

The street outside The Viper Room became a shrine to River Phoenix,
with fans and admirers travelling from far and wide to mark the site where
the actor died.

Many laid flowers. Incense burned and the walls and doors were
adorned with scribbled chalk notices, all aimed at commemorating River
Phoenix. Inscribed in blue and gold chalk was the phrase 'The Eternal River
Flows' on a watercolour, left beside the spontaneous pavement altar to the
fallen star. Another inscription read 'a true individual who will be remembered'.

While most of the offerings were heartfelt expressions of grief at the loss of Phoenix, this being Hollywood, some could not resist the chance that publicity might help their careers, no matter how macabre the means. One aspiring actress named Missy had attached an eight-by-ten head shot of herself to a condolences note and a bunch of flowers. Similarly, now that there was a vacancy in *Interview With The Vampire*, which River Phoenix had been due to start in the last week of November, producer Stephen Woolley found his desk inundated with faxes on the Monday morning after Phoenix's death from aspiring actors looking to fill the part before the actual cause of death of the young actor had even been determined. It was nothing more or less than an opportunity to the out-of-work acting fraternity in Hollywood.

River Phoenix's body was returned to his family home in Gainesville in a blue coffin. The Phoenix family tried to keep the final viewing of River's body secret, but nevertheless 60 people turned up to mourn the star. His brother Joaquin (Leaf) was reported by mourners to have said words of praise for River's life and expressed sadness that it was so brief.

Phoenix lay in his coffin, dressed in a black Aleka's Attic T shirt. Around

The sidewalk outside the Viper Room on Sunset Strip became a spontaneous shrine to the memory of River Phoenix.

his neck hung several necklaces and beads. His shoulder length hair, dyed black for his role in *Dark Blood*, was cut short and the cuttings placed next to Phoenix in the coffin, reportedly at his mother's request. Arlyn Phoenix placed a single pink carnation by her son's left shoulder, accompanied by Samantha Mathis. Arrangements were made to have his body cremated and his ashes buried near the family home in Gainesville, Florida.

Several of Phoenix's friends and colleagues attended a memorial service, also held in Gainesville, including his agent Iris Burton, musicians Flea and Michael Stipe from REM, as well as actor Dan Aykroyd, whom Phoenix had starred beside in *Sneakers*. Aykroyd had reportedly been aware of Phoenix's growing drug use and had made several attempts to warn the young actor, particularly given the example of Aykroyd's *Blues Brothers* co-star John Belushi. There was an unusual musical accompaniment to this memorial service - the demo tracks River Phoenix had recorded with his band Aleka's Attic. There was apparently singing and dancing in the dead star's honour, echoing the funeral scene at the end of *My Own Private Idaho* .

On Thursday 25th November an official Hollywood memorial service was held. Among those in attendance were Peter Bogdanovich, director of *The Thing Called Love* , Rob Reiner, director of *Stand By Me* , actress Helen Mirren, who appeared alongside Phoenix in *The Mosquito Coast*, actress Christine Lahti, from *Running On Empty*, screenwriter Naomi Foner, Phoenix's last Hollywood agent Iris Burton, his sisters Rain, Liberty, and Summer. Arlyn spoke some words in tribute, and then laid her son to rest. Joaquin (Leaf) and father John stayed in Florida with the ashes.

In a letter to *The Los Angeles Times*, published on 24th November, Arlyn Phoenix offered her explanation for the untimely end that had befallen her son, and responded to the many press reports that had followed his death on Halloween.

'River was not a regular drug user,' wrote Arlyn. 'He lived at home in Florida with us and was almost never a part of the "club scene" in Los Angeles. He had just arrived in LA from the pristine beauty and quietness of Utah, where he was filming for six weeks. We feel that the excitement and energy of the Halloween night-club and party scene were way beyond his usual experience and control...'

Other family members also gave their reactions to the media. Only two days after Phoenix's death, his grandmother Margaret Dunetz reportedly could not believe the news, speaking of her grandson in the present tense: 'I'm still in shock. I can't describe what a wonderful kid he is. I can't understand why - how - it could happen.'

Phoenix's publicist Susan Patricola was also confronted by many reporters about her client's supposed commitment to 'clean living'. How could this stance be squared by the actor's death from a seemingly self-administered drug overdose? 'It wasn't about clean living,' she said defensively of her late client's lifestyle. 'It was about not killing animals, not eating or wearing anything that came from an animal. That doesn't even play into clean living.' Sky Sworski, a longtime friend of Phoenix and occasionally band manager for Aleka's Attic said: 'I know one thing: River did not want to die. That's pretty much all I can say. He had too much going on. He wasn't an addict, that's for sure. He dabbled. He kept it from me, because there would have been trouble. He was pretty secretive about it. It's a release. People find different ways of escaping - he had a lot of stress, not only on the set.'

Speculation mounted that River Phoenix may have done his greatest service to the world in dying the way he did. Many took the opportunity of the star's dramatic fall from grace to highlight an anti-drug message, hoping that the implications of drug-taking would sink into the audience that had built up around Phoenix. 'Hopefully it's a wake up call to the world,' said Susan Patricola. 'It leaves you to question why young people are compelled to do this.'

A photographer from *The Enquirer* managed to snatch a picture of the unfortunate actor in his coffin, which was splashed in full colour across the centre spread of the scandal-mongering magazine. The excuse the publication used was one of warning. The accompanying account of River Phoenix's funeral quoted one Dr Merle E. Parker, president of the national organisation War on Drugs saying: 'The picture of River Phoenix, in his coffin at age 23, says all that needs to be said about illegal drug use. Use drugs and you'll end up just like River - in a casket. Hollywood stars always seem to be glamorising drug use. But this photo shows that drugs aren't glamorous at all. *The Enquirer* is doing a public service by publishing it. It shows what drug use is really all about - it's about death.'

That kind of coverage prompted many newspapers to send their journalists down to clubs like The Viper Room to see if the impact of Phoenix's death had caused anyone to change their behaviour - to ease up on the drug taking. Most journalists discovered that the scene was much the same as ever, and reported the fact in sensational terms. Under the headline 'River's dead but hey...that don't mean we can't get out of our heads', British tabloid newspaper *The Sun* concocted a 'shock expose' piece, published on 27th November. The reporter, Caroline Graham, wrote: 'Inside the club where [River] Phoenix spent his final few hours it's business as usual...'

And, indeed it was, according to one anonymous funster: 'I knew River, but hey - he's gone. Why should that stop me from having a good time? He lived cool, he died cool. He'd want us to carry on having fun in his memory.'

Phoenix received more considered tributes from some of the actors and actresses he worked with, among them Harrison Ford, who said he had been 'proud to watch him grow into a man of such talent, integrity and compassion'.

1970 – 31 OCTOBER 1993

...nsider myself an ... Sort of an Arnold ...warzenegger with ... a Nigel Tufnel (from *Spinal Tap*) twist. I walk ... close to the edges. I ... kiss them with my toe."

"In Florida I used to sing with my brothers and sisters in talent shows, winning prize after prize — we thought that we were going to be the next Jackson Five!"

"My name used to be Rio when we lived in South America — it was taken from Herman Hesse's *Siddhartha*; my middle name is Jude from the Beatles song."

river on river

"What I'm really concerned with is the air, the water, the earth that we live on. It's had enough and at this rate, poetry won't last, good movies won't last."

"In my Utopic world I'd live on a tropical island before any industrialisation and pollution; I'd be able to fly up to a mountain range nearby where there was snow, then make a sled out of an old stump and ski down the mountain to the bottom, where I could bathe and swim in a running river and meet up with a group of friends. Life would be nicer if I could fly like Peter Pan."

"I think Keanu and I are the nicest guys on the planet – with the exception of George Bush and Ronald Reagan."

"When we left South America we had no money. So a priest got us on his old Tonka freighter that carried Tonka toys. We were stowaways. The crew discovered us half way home – my mom threw a big birthday party for my brother, gave us all these damaged Tonka toys – it was a blast."

"I love my name but when I was 11, yeah, I wanted to change it to Scott or Steve."

"Sometimes I'll hear stuff like 'Hey, man, where's your skateboard, dude?' from people who think I'm Christian Slater."

"I believe in all life, from trees to mice to men."

SKY MAGAZINE - 87

NATIONAL ENQUIRER

LARGEST CIRCULATION OF ANY PAPER IN AMERICA

ENQUIRER PHOTO SPECIAL

70p November 16, 1993
U.S. $1.75, Canada $1.29, Austria 2.30, Denmark Kr. 14.50, France F 10.00, Germany DM 3.80, Italy L 3,500, The Netherlands L99, Spain Ptas. 325

BORN 1970   DIED 1993

RIVER PHOENIX TRAGEDY

THE UNTOLD STORY of movie idol's final nightmarish hours

DIANA ROSS: THE TRUTH ABOUT MY CHILD'S FATHER

The 18-year secret she kept out of her book

'RISING SUN' STAR WESLEY SNIPES BEATEN TO A PULP

Snipes in his new movie, 'Demolition Man'

— by his own bodyguard

UPSETS FOR CHEERS STARS
WHOOPI DUMPS DANSON

KIRSTIE OUTRAGED AFTER GAY PAINTS HER HUBBY NAKED

SUPER MODEL CINDY PROVES SHE'S A REAL TURKISH DELIGHT

the death of RIVER PHOENIX

The enigmatic River Phoenix was always known as one of young Hollywood's clean and sober brigade, and one of its more intense anti-drugs spokesmen, chiding his peers at the first hint of mildly hedonistic behaviour. Then he died, just 23 years old, and suddenly the Hollywood rumour mill ground into overtime. John Voland reports from Los Angeles . . . ▷

OUTLINE

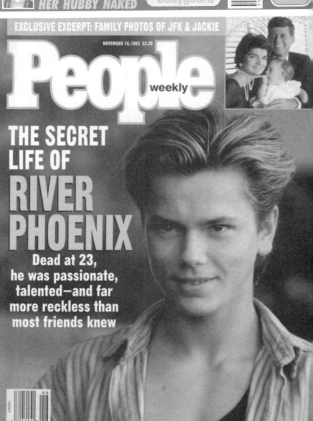

EXCLUSIVE EXCERPT: FAMILY PHOTOS OF JFK & JACKIE

NOVEMBER 16, 1993 $2.20

People weekly

THE SECRET LIFE OF RIVER PHOENIX

Dead at 23, he was passionate, talented—and far more reckless than most friends knew

46

A DOUBLE LIFE
THE TRUTH ABOUT RIVER
PHOENIX, BY IAN PARKER

ROBERT FISK O...
WHY TELEVISION CAN'T
COPE WITH REALITY

PLUS NELSON MANDELA O...
MUHAMMAD ALI A STUD...
OF ANJELICA HUSTON...
AND WHY GOOSE FAT I...
GOOD FOR YO...

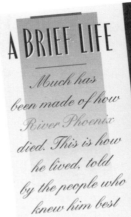

A BRIEF LIFE

Much has been made of how River Phoenix died. This is how he lived, told by the people who knew him best

An Oral History

MAGAZINE

LOST BOYS

River Phoenix and the tribe he left behind

PLUS:
Charles Bremner
Ben MacIntyre
Robert Crampton
Rose Tremain

A couple of weeks before he died, Just 17 talked to River. This is one of the last interviews he ever gave.

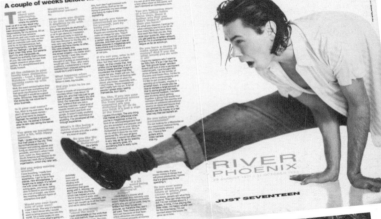

RIVER PHOENIX

JUST SEVENTEEN

Weekend
The Guardian

HOLLYWOOD BABYLON

RIVER'S END

Actor River Phoenix was young, idealistic and full of promise. His death at 23 stunned friends—and revealed a dark side that few knew existed

the viper room

His *I Love You To Death* co-star, Miriam Margolyes, called Phoenix 'an honourable young man. Gentle, genuine, a roaring talent. His death is a great loss.'

The media reaction was astonishing, removing from the Hollywood headlines the death of Italian film director Frederico Fellini, whom most would consider a much more significant figure in the world of cinema. Fellini's death, which occurred on the same day as River Phoenix, was expected - he was 73 and had been ill and even in a coma for some time. His working life was clearly behind him and his best film work had been produced long ago. Phoenix, however, was young, and clearly his best was yet to come. His death was sudden, shocking, mysterious and unexpected, just the kind of thing to grab the headlines. Within days, however, the Phoenix story had been succeeded by the California fires which were devastating rich housing areas inhabited by many Hollywood stars. Such are the vagaries of the news machine.

Commenting on the Phoenix story at its height on TV, *Variety* columnist Amy Archerd said: 'There hasn't been anything this catastrophic and dramatic since James Dean and Natalie Wood died.' Others weren't so taken with the death of this promising young actor. Rush Limbaugh, a right-wing TV and radio chat show host, who had recently found notoriety in the United States through his habit of making outrageous statements on air, was almost the only dissenting voice: 'From the moment his death was discovered, you would have thought the President of the United States had been murdered here...that we've lost some great contributor to the social and human condition. This guy - look at his name! River Phoenix! He's the son of a couple of whacked out hippies.'

Naturally, Phoenix's fraternity of teen female fans went into days of mourning following his death. *The Sunday Times* in Britain carried a report from Serena Gilbert, a pupil at Cheney School, Oxford, on her classmates reaction to the news. 'Some feel as though a lover has been taken away from them. Phoenix was the boy most girls wanted to have as a boyfriend. "It seems," one girl said, "that River has disappeared as quickly as he came".'

Teen magazines were quick to produce tributes to their young readers' fallen idol, illustrated with many moody photos of the young star and the usual, relevant environmentally friendly quotes. But while schoolgirls around the world mourned for one of their pin-up idols, other groups were trying to reclaim the Phoenix image for themselves. The gay subculture was one that had latched onto Phoenix as an image reflecting their lifestyles. In its obituary for Phoenix, *The Modern Review* ('Low Culture for High Brows') pointed this out. 'Thanks to his ephebian looks and in particular to his little-rent-boy-lost routine in *[My Own Private] Idaho*, Phoenix is also likely to be remembered as a bona fide gay pin up. Especially endearing to gays is the fact that Phoenix himself re-wrote the script of *Idaho* to make his character's inversion more overt. Clear proof of Phoenix's iconic fame among homosexuals came when heterosexual homophile Brett Anderson [of the band Suede] was asked by an NME questionnaire: "Who is sexy?" His studied reply was River Phoenix. The homosexual element in Phoenix's fan club was ignored however by "human interest" press coverage of his death, which preferred to concentrate on all-girls schools, where blubbing fourth-formers reminded us of Phoenix's commendable stance on environmental issues.'

Britain's *Gay Times* marked Phoenix's passing with a full page in its December 1993 issue, in which Mark Simpson tried to sum up Phoenix's appeal to the gay community. 'Phoenix on screen had a presence very much as that described by Richard Dyer in his account of the gay investment in stars such as Montgomery Clift and Dirk Bogarde: that of the "Sad Young Man", the outsider male who seemed different, lonely, wounded - searching for something that might heal him or give meaning to his "queer" existence.'

In addition, Simpson speculated on the Phoenix-Dean connection which was gaining further currency in the media and the popular imagination. 'Dean and Phoenix did share something in life that early death unites them in: a proud, if tragic, resistance to the responsibilities of adulthood. Dean was both presented and taken away from us an adolescent; Phoenix was a boy we had watched grow up painfully, but never quite make it to manhood. Both refused to become men and in death this refusal becomes eternal.'

Phoenix was due back at work the following week on the interior studio sets of *Dark Blood*, to shoot the vital scenes between the three principal characters set within the hut where Boy lived. The production was shut down upon the news of Phoenix's death, while British producers Nik Powell and Joanne Sellars assessed their options. 'There aren't many next moves,' said Powell, who was doubtful that the film could ever be completed. 'With three weeks left in production and many major scenes to be shot, it is near impossible to complete the film without River Phoenix,' he said, preparing to abandon the project. Concerning Phoenix's drug use, Powell was guarded: 'Our information was - and still is - that he was a clean-living kid.'

There was speculation that the Completion Bond company would take a dim view of the film languishing uncompleted. Completion Bond companies provide the last batch of finance for many independent films, with strings attached. Often Bond companies can take over productions if schedules are slipping or the production is experiencing difficulties. Their main aim is to ensure a financial return for investors in the film, and if that means sacking a director or replacing a lead actor to ensure the film is finished and released that's what they'll do.

In the case of *Dark Blood*, however, it would be very difficult to get anything resembling a finished film from the footage shot prior to Phoenix's death. Using a stand-in or double in major dialogue and character scenes was just not feasible. However, financial institutions underwriting films can insist that something is released, as it is only with a finished product out in the market place that the investors have a chance of making any of their investment back. It is yet possible that some of Phoenix's work on *Dark Blood* may yet be seen, in one form or another, if the film can be reworked somehow.

However, the performance that River Phoenix was gearing up to give in *Interview With The Vampire* (1994) will have to remain in the imaginations of his fans, as nothing had been shot featuring Phoenix at the time of his death. River Phoenix had been cast in the small but pivotal role of the interviewer in the film version of the 1976 novel by Anne Rice. The film project had been circulating Hollywood for over a decade before the team behind the controversial surprise hit *The Crying Game* (1993) - Neil Jordan and ex-Palace Pictures executives Nik Powell and Stephen Woolley - managed to get the project underway. Irishman Neil Jordan was quickly confirmed as director on the newly kick-started project.

Interview With The Vampire cast Brad Pitt as a vampire named Louis who was to be seen telling all to Phoenix as the interviewer, named Daniel in one of Anne Rice's follow-up novels. Controversially cast in the central role of the vampire Lestat was Tom Cruise, deemed by many fans of the original book an unsuitable choice. Cruise took on the role after Daniel Day Lewis had rejected it in a previous incarnation of the project.

Before his death, Phoenix did talk to American *Premiere* about his role. He seemed strangely unenthusiastic about the project. 'I don't like vampires all that much,' he claimed. 'I find them to be full of shit, frankly. It's good that they cast me as the interviewer in the sense that I can be pessimistic.'

The script, by Neil Jordan and original author Anne Rice, puts as much emphasis on the erotic as on the gore, which caused Phoenix some problems with the role. 'It's weird when you see erotic stuff back-to-back with blood and stuff. I'm sure in the realm of vampires, it's very sexy.'

Shooting in San Francisco was just about complete when River Phoenix died. He was due to begin shooting the interviewer segment on 30th November, immediately after wrapping production on *Dark Blood*. After the actor's death, the part was quickly recast with Christian Slater in the role. Slater decided to donate his income to River Phoenix's favourite environmental charities, which included Earth Save in Santa Cruz and Earth Trust in Malibu. 'That's the only way I could have done it,' said Slater. 'When I first heard about it, after getting over the initial shock, I thought, oh God, who are they going to get?'

Stephen Woolley, the producer of *Interview With The Vampire*, had only one comment to make on the death of his prospective cast member: 'Most people between the ages of eighteen and 25 take drugs.' River Phoenix would never see the age of 25. He was 23 and dead - all those prospects for the great performances to come gone with him. There had already been other projects talked about in the last year of his life. John Boorman had considered casting him in *Broken Dreams* as a young man on a quest to find objects his conjurer father made disappear. Boorman co-wrote the screenplay with *Interview With The Vampire*'s Neil Jordan, and hoped to have Sean Connery starring as the father and Winona Ryder also in the cast.

Christopher Hampton, the playwright who wrote *Dangerous Liaisons*, had completed a script to feature Phoenix alongside John Malkovich in *Total Eclipse*, a tale of a gay couple mired in a fatal relationship. The German director Volker Schlorndorff was lined up to direct. There were many other properties that Phoenix had expressed an interest in prior to his death which would have been very different films for Phoenix's involvement.

'He was all set to work right through to his 30th birthday,' said an employee in the offices of Phoenix's attorney, Eric Greenspan. 'It's really, really sad.'

River Phoenix: a tragic life cut short before his talent could reach its full potential.

Filmography

Various commercials for products including Ocean Spray, Saks and Mitsubishi

Real Kids (1980)
Performed as an audience warm up act with sister Rain.

Fantasy (1980)
Performed musical items on kids variety show.

Seven Brides For Seven Brothers (1982-83) USA 1982 1 x 90 min, 21 x 60 mins. Broadcast on NBC, 19th September 1982 to 23rd March 1983. Episodes directed by Gary Nelson (pilot), James Sheldon, Harvey S. Laidman, Barry Crane, John Patterson and others. Written by Sue Grafton & Steven Humphrey (pilot), Marshall Herskovitz, Mitzie Marvin, Jud Scott, Earl W. Wallace and others. Production Company: MGM/UA Entertainment Ltd and David Gerber.
Cast: Richard Dean Anderson (Adam), Roger Wilson (Daniel), Peter Horton (Crane), Drake Hogestyn (Brian), Bryan Utman (Ford), Tim Topper (Evan), River Phoenix (Guthrie), Terri Treas (Hannah)

Celebrity (1984) USA 1984 3 x 120 minutes. Broadcast on NBC over 12th, 13th and 14th February 1984. Directed by Paul Wendkos. Screenplay by William

Hanley. Based on the novel by Thomas Thompson. Production Company: NBC. Producer Rosilyn Heller. Co-Producer: Richard L. O'Connor. Director of Photography: Philip Lathrop, ASC. Original Music: Leonard Rosenman
Cast: Michael Beck (T. J. Lowther), Ben Masters (Kleber Cantrell), Joseph Bottoms (Mac Crawford), Hal Holbrook (Calvin Sledge), River Phoenix (Jeffie, aged 11)

It's Your Move (1984) USA 1984 30 minutes. Broadcast NBC 26th September 1984. River Pheonix played Brian in the first five minutes only of this pilot for a TV series. He had one line of dialogue.

Hotel
Broadcast ABC September 1983 to August 1988. River Phoenix featured in an episode of this on-going drama

Robert Kennedy and His Times (1985) USA 1985 3 x 140 mins. Broadcast CBS over 27th, 28th, 29th January 1985. Directed by Marvin J. Chomsky. Screenplay by Walon Green. Based on the book by Arthur M. Schlesinger Jr.
Cast: Brad Davis (Robert Kennedy), Veronica Cartwright (Ethel Kennedy), Jack Warden (Joseph Kennedy Sr), Jason Bateman (Joe III), Shannon Doherty (Kathleen), River Phoenix (Robert Kennedy Jr). River Phoenix only appeared in Part 3 of the series

Backwards: The Riddle of Dyslexia
After-school educational special, which featured River Phoenix

Family Ties (1985)
USA 1982-1989 30 minute episodes Broadcast NBC 14th November 1985 River Phoenix featured as Eugene Forbes in the episode 'My Tutor'

Surviving: A Family in Crisis (1985)
USA 1985 120 minutes, made for TV movie. Broadcast ABC 10th February 1985. Directed by Waris Hussein. Screenplay by Joyce Eliason

Cast: Ellen Burstyn (Tina Brogan), Len Cariou (David Brogan), Zach Galligan (Rick Brogan), Marsha Mason (Lois), Molly Ringwald (Lonnie), Paul Sorvino (Harvey), River Phoenix (Philip Brogan), Heather O'Rourke (Sarah Brogan)

Explorers (1985)
USA 1985 110 minutes. Directed by Joe Dante. Screenplay by Eric Luke. Production Company: Paramount Pictures.
Cast: Ethan Hawke (Ben Crandall), River Phoenix (Wolfgang Muller), Jason Presson (Darren Woods), Amanda Peterson (Lori Swenson), Dick Miller (Charlie Drake), Robert Picardo (Wak/Starkiller), Leslie Rickert (Neek)

Stand By Me (1986)
USA 1986 85 minutes. Directed by Rob Reiner. Screenplay by Raynold Gideon & Bruce A. Evans. Based upon the novella *The Body* by Stephen King. Production Company: Columbia.
Cast: Wil Wheaton (Gordie Lachance), River Phoenix (Chris Chambers), Corey Feldman (Teddy Duchamp), Jerry O'Connell (Vern Tessio), Richard Dreyfuss (The Writer), Kiefer Sutherland (Ace Merrill)

The Mosquito Coast (1986)
USA 1986 117 minutes. Directed by Peter Weir. Screenplay by Paul Schrader. Production Company: Saul Zaentz.
Cast: Harrison Ford (Allie Fox), Helen Mirren (Mother), River Phoenix (Charlie), Jadrien Steele (Jerry), Hilary Gordon (April), Rebecca Gordon (Clover), Andre Gregory (Reverend Spellgood), Melanie Boland (Mrs Spellgood), Martha Plimpton (Emily Spellgood)

A Night in the Life of Jimmy Reardon (1988) UK Title: Jimmy Reardon
USA 1988 93 minutes. Directed by 'William Richert. Screenplay by William Richert. Based on the novel *Aren't You Even Gonna Kiss Me Goodbye*, by William Richert. Production Company: Island Pictures.
Cast: River Phoenix (Jimmy Reardon), Ann Magnuson (Joyce Fickett), Meredith Salenger (Lisa Bentwright), Ione Skye (Denise Hunter), Louanne (Suzie Middleberg), Matthew L. Perry (Fred Roberts), Paul Koslo (Al Reardon), Jane Hallaren (Faye Reardon)

Little Nikita (1988)
USA 1988 98 minutes. Directed by Richard Benjamin. Screenplay by John Hill and Bo Goldman. Based on a story by Tom Musca & Terry Schwartz. Production Company: Columbia.
Cast: Sidney Poitier (Roy Parmenter), River Phoenix (Jeff Grant), Richard Jenkins (Richard Grant), Caroline Kava (Elizabeth Grant), Richard Bradford (Konstantin Karpov), Loretta Devine (Verna McLaughlin)

Running on Empty (1988)
USA 1988 118 minutes. Directed by Sidney Lumet. Screenplay by Naomi Foner. Production Company: Lorimar Film Entertainment.
Cast: Christine Lahti (Annie Pope), River Phoenix (Danny Pope), Judd Hirsch (Arthur Pope), Jonas Abry (Harry Pope), Martha Plimpton (Lorna Philips), Ed Crowley (Mr Philips)

Indiana Jones and the Last Crusade (1989)
USA 1989 127 minutes. Directed by Steven Spielberg. Screenplay by Jeffrey Boam, based on a story by George Lucas, Menno Meyjes. Based on characters created by George Lucas, Philip Kaufman. Production Company: Lucasfilm, for Paramount.
Cast: Harrison Ford (Indiana Jones), Sean Connery (Dr Henry Jones), Den-

holm Elliott (Marcus Brody), Alison Doody (Dr Elsa Schneider), John Rhys-Davies (Sallah), Julian Glover (Walter Donovan), River Phoenix (Young Indy)

I Love You To Death (1990)

USA 1990 97 minutes. Directed by Lawrence Kasdan. Screenplay by John Kostmayer. Production Company: Tri-Star.

Cast: Kevin Kline (Joey Boca), Tracey Ullman (Rosaline Boca), Joan Plowright (Nadja), River Phoenix (Devo), William Hurt (Harlan James), Keanu Reeves (Marlon James)

Dogfight (1991)

USA 1991 92 minutes. Directed by Nancy Savoca. Screenplay by Bob Comfort. Production Company: Warner Brothers.

Cast: River Phoenix (Birdlace), Lili Taylor (Rose), Richard Panebranco (Berzine), Anthony Clark (Oxie), Mitchell Whitfield (Benjamin), Holly Near (Rose Snr), E. G. Daily (Marcie), Sue Morales (Ruth Two Bears)

My Own Private Idaho (1991)

USA 1991 114 minutes, Directed by Gus Van Sant. Screenplay by Gus Van Sant, additional dialogue by William Shakespeare. Production Company: New Line Cinema.

Cast: River Phoenix (Mike Waters), Keanu Reeves (Scott Favor), James Russo (Richard Waters), William Richert (Bob Pigeon), Rodney Harvey (Gary), Chiara Caselli (Carmella), Michael Parker (Digger), Jessie Thomas (Denise), Flea (Budd), Grace Zabriskie (Alena), Tom Troupe (Jack Favor)

Sneakers (1992)

USA 1992 125 minutes. Directed by Phil Alden Robinson. Screenplay by Phil Alden Robinson, Lawrence Lasker, Walter F. Parkes. Production Company: Universal Pictures.

Cast: Robert Redford (Martin Bishop), Dan Aykroyd ('Mother'), Ben Kingsley (Cosmo), Mary McDonnell (Liz), River

Phoenix (Carl), Sidney Poitier (Crease)

Silent Tongue (1993)

USA 1992 106 minutes. Directed by Sam Shepard. Screenplay by Sam Shepard. Production Company: Belbo Films/ Alive Films.

Cast: Richard Harris (Prescott Roe), Sheila Tousey (Awbonnie/Ghost), Alan Bates (Eamon McCree), River Phoenix (Talbot Roe), Dermot Mulroney (Reeves McCree), Jeri Arredondo (Velada McCree), Tantoo Cardinal (Silent Tongue)

The Thing Called Love (1993)

USA 1993 92 minutes. Directed by Peter Bogdanovich. Production Company: Paramount Pictures.

Cast: River Phoenix (James Wright), Samantha Mathis (Miranda), Kyle (Dermot Mulroney)

Uncompleted Films and Cameo Appearances

Even Cowgirls Get The Blues (1993, Gus Van Sant)

Small cameo role as a guru-seeking hippy.

Dark Blood (1993, George Sluizer)

Cast as Boy, alongside Judy Davis and Jonathan Pryce. The film is unlikely to be completed as many of Phoenix's important scenes with the two other principals remained unshot at the time of his death.

Interview With The Vampire (1994 Neil Jordan)

Phoenix had been cast in the small, but central, role of the Interviewer in Neil Jordan's version of the cult Anne Rice novel which stars Tom Cruise as the vampire Lestat. Christian Slater replaced Phoenix in the role.

Learning Resource Centre Stockton Riverside College